Christians
in School?

Taking the good news to today's schools.

CHRISTIANS IN SCHOOL?

'Tricia Williams

Scripture Union
130 City Road, London EC1V 2NJ

First published 1985

ISBN 0 86201 309 7

All Scripture quotations, except where stated, are taken from the New International Version © 1978 by New York International Bible Society.

Phototypeset by Wyvern Typesetting Limited, Bristol

Printed and bound in Great Britain by
Cox & Wyman Ltd, Reading

Contents

Introduction

Everyone goes to school. It affects all of us. It shapes our lives and our society. Even if we left school years ago, it still affects our tomorrow. Think of school and you think of the young. This book is about the young and the school environment that is moulding them. It's about the pressures they face in a world without God. It's about young disciples who are obeying Jesus' command to be his witnesses; and it's about the opportunities and challenge the schools of today present to the church.

As well as being a schools worker with Scripture Union for several years, I have taught in both a comprehensive school and an independent, co-educational boarding school. During all that time, it has been a privilege to meet with and learn from hundreds of Christian teenagers and teachers who are wholeheartedly committed to living for Christ in the mission field where God has placed them – school.

I hope that you will be challenged by them and learn from them as I have.

'Tricia Williams, Autumn 1984.

'My prayer is not that you take them out of the world but that you protect them from the evil one. . . . As you sent me into the world, I have sent them into the world' (John 17:15, 18).

1

The task

Scruffy, chipped school doors opened into an untidy corridor. Noise and people were everywhere; people shouting to be heard; people running and pushing, going nowhere in particular. Frequently my companion and I had to stand against the wall as teenagers forced their way through. No one seemed to notice us. There was an air of frantic activity. Bags, books, sweet-papers and coats were left abandoned and trampled. This was my welcome on a visit to a large comprehensive school in the south of England.

Underground Christians

My guide through this maze was a tall girl of about sixteen. Her manner was pleasant and there was a strength about her, but also a quiet resignation. We struggled up stairs through the masses, past noticeboards covered in graffiti and walls in need of a good coat of paint. At last we reached an out-of-the-way classroom and opened the door on a different world.

Outside, the school seemed full of noise, hostile faces and disturbance. In this dusty little room where the sun shone in showing up the desk carvings to their best advantage, there was peace. Twenty-five faces turned towards us. This was the Christian Union.

The group was made up of both boys and girls, ages ranging from about fourteen to seventeen. There was a quiet burble of conversation as people talked and listened and shared lunch together. The contrast with the world outside this room was stark. They knew I was a Christian, but to begin with there was a wariness in their eyes as though they found it difficult to trust anyone from outside their group. In the midst of this intensely secular environment, their ties of friendship and fellowship were strong. For them the Christian Union was the rock which allowed survival in a very turbulent and often frightening world. There was a defensiveness about the group. Their struggle made them suspicious, even of visiting Christians.

At the end of lunchtime, back in the car, it felt almost as if I had just emerged from an underground church. This was a tough school. How then was it that up to thirty teenagers chose to meet together regularly to talk about their faith in Jesus Christ and to encourage one another, with no adult support inside school? Even though I was saddened by their understandable fortress mentality, the resolute faith of this young group deserved respect.

The look in the eyes of these teenagers had said: 'You don't know what it's like living in this school as a Christian.' They were right. I walked out of the oppressive atmosphere one hour after arriving and left it behind. They have to live there every day. It was humbling to be reminded of how God works; here in the most unpromising of places was this good sized group of teenagers who chose to meet together because of their iron-hard faith, with no teachers to help them, no official encouragement and no adult ideas for 'meetings'.

This particularly unwelcoming comprehensive is, of course, not typical of all our schools. Many are well-run, happy establishments where there are good relationships between well-motivated pupils and caring teaching staff. However, the needs and pressures in that school are reflected in more subtle ways elsewhere.

Counting the cost

On another visit to an apparently well-ordered, comfortable school, I talked with the Christian group about sharing their faith in school, perhaps making a start by offering to take assembly. The reaction in the room was electric. They were horrified and afraid of this superficially simple, everyday challenge. Cosy as the school might seem, it was a place where those who dared own the Christian faith were held in contempt by their fellows. One of the boys was the son of a local minister. His father had recently been invited to take an assembly at the school. The boy was so afraid of the mocking that he knew would follow, that he begged his father to telephone the headmaster and cancel the arrangement. Later, some Christians from the same school described how as they had been going to a CU meeting, non-Christian teenagers had thrown stones at them – a latter-day stoning for the Christian faith! This little group was understandably full of fear.

Teenagers can be outspoken and often lack sensitivity towards other individuals. Establishing yourself as a person in the world and being accepted by those of your own age-group are all-important and to be a Christian teenager in a hostile world of unbelieving young people can be an extremely painful experience. Adults are usually polite with each other or straightforwardly apathetic. The world of young people has a harsh reality and honesty about it and for Christian young people there is no easy way. The choice is often stark: count the cost and suffer for your faith or give up.

Society without God

We live in a Godless society; a society in which God's name has largely been forgotten and for the present generation is just another swear-word; a society where values have been turned upside down, where those who demonstrate against the destructive power of nuclear arms also demonstrate for the right to kill their unborn children; a society where there is no right or wrong, except mine, where every man does what is right in his own eyes; a society where, as a result, there is discontent, a sense of loss, insidious fear and hatred.

Somehow, perhaps remembering our own school days, we expect school to be a haven of morality and uprightness, a last outpost of a once 'Christian' society. But with the majority of schools being run by those who would not claim a Christian faith, curricula planned by non-Christians, agnostic teachers in the classroom, not to mention the pupils – thousands of young people who never set foot inside a church – we should not be surprised that often the school community is simply a reflection of the confused and Godless society of which it is a part.

Christian adults have learnt to live with the contrast of values which exists between those of the Christian community and those of the world. In churches and Christian families the rule of God is accepted; in the world it is rejected. Adults have had time to discover how to cope, one way or another, with the conflict which this creates in their own individual lives and in their relationships with others. For Christian teenagers the battle is sharp and new, and therefore infinitely greater.

At a time when they are expending an enormous amount of energy simply in the struggle of growing up, and when impressing their peers and being one of the crowd is so important, young Christians also have to come to terms with the realisation that they must stand out from the crowd and that often this will mean rejection by classmates. How much they need the loving support of the rest of the Body of Christ!

Opportunities

Does this seem a black picture? In some ways it is. Our nation has turned from God, and the biblical principle of the sins of the parents affecting their children is working itself out. Our young people are confused and struggling with sins they are not sure if they have committed, because no one will admit to them when sin is sin. But in the midst of this darkness there are tremendous opportunities.

Everyone goes to school. Practically the whole of a generation from one community is brought together in the secondary school for five to seven years. At no other time of life does this happen. A whole generation on the church's doorstep; what an opportunity! All too often our twentieth-century western thinking is too isolationist. We think of a local church only in terms of the meetings that happen in the building. Have we, perhaps, taken the biblical picture of the church as a building too literally? As a result we fail to see ourselves as having a corporate responsibility to serve and share the gospel with those who never enter a church building or attend a service. We often fail to think about the locality God has called us to live in or talk about it with other Christian brothers and sisters from different denominations in the same area or town. We need to pray together and plan strategically. The local school is a part of our local community and in addition to providing an immense opportunity for sharing the good news of Jesus Christ, it is also an immense responsibility.

For young Christians in particular there is an exciting and challenging call to answer. Jesus Christ calls them to be his 'witnesses . . . to the ends of the earth'. For them that means school: that is where they spend most of their waking hours. Costly it may be, but as many young disciples have discovered, living for Jesus Christ at school brings an urgency to life, a sense of purpose and responsibility, a reality to a world which is full of make-believe. In short, Jesus brings an abundance of life which other young people lack. The Christian faith is not meant to be put in a Sunday-only box, but shared liberally in every way with others at school.

Some of those Christians who had stones thrown at them came to an inter-school meeting for Christian Union members a few months later. No longer did they seem afraid. Their faces had changed. They talked eagerly about what God was doing in their school; they were excited and expectant. God had challenged them about their witness and they had decided that in spite of their fears, they would begin to reach out to non-Christians, inviting them to their meetings and talking openly about their faith in Christ. Things had not become easier in one sense. They were still subjected to unkind teasing, but with the Holy Spirit's help they had discovered that their fears didn't matter. Through sharing their faith they were becoming stronger, not weaker.

The young Christians in our churches are the best resource we have for evangelism amongst school-age teenagers. Every week thousands of churches send out their Christian young people into needy schools. Day by day they are meeting with hundreds of non-Christians; for several years they have the opportunity to live out the Christian life in front of many who may never meet another real believer or set foot inside a church.

Many young Christians who are much in evidence at the Sunday night youth fellowship, keep a low profile when it comes to Monday morning at school. It's not only the Christian teachers who are discouraged by this, it is also pupils. For example, there was a small group of girls in a Bristol school who struggled to meet regularly to pray; they would have greatly valued the fellowship and support of Christian boys who were at the same school but who didn't come because of the risk of being thought weak for going to a Christian meeting. In another school there was a Christian Union of ten people. There could have been fifty, if the other forty who attended the Saturday night Christian concerts had also understood the importance of meeting with others in school to share the burdens of discipleship where it counted, rather than just wanting to be part of an audience.

Churches have often failed to capitalise on this huge missionary force. Young Christians have wrongly been seen as the church of the future rather than recognising them as part of the Body of Christ now. As such, they have responsibilities too. Instead of giving young people an awareness of this we have actively taken it away from them, teaching by implication that evangelism is something that is done *to* them or *for* them or to entertain them by outsiders. We have not challenged them to see that Christ commands them also to 'go and make disciples . . .' Of course this does not mean that outside speakers, music and drama groups have no place in schools evangelism. We must take whatever opportunities there are. Instead these efforts should be seen as supporting the ministry of Christians who are already in place and have the task of demonstrating that the Christian faith is not just about words and ideas but about actions and changed lives. Unintentionally, twentieth-century evangelicals have failed to teach young Christians that the lordship of Christ isn't an optional extra.

Teenagers may not have the maturity or depth of teaching of older Christians, but they are still the ones who are best equipped to communicate with their peers at school. They speak the language, they understand the trends in fashion and music; they share the same concerns and interests. If a teenager at school is converted and starts living for Jesus, people notice.

Kevin is a Christian sixth former from Devon. One of his teachers described him. Kevin had been one of the first punks and was well-known by teachers and pupils alike as he seemed to spend most of his days sitting outside the headmaster's office. Then in the third year he was converted. Overnight, he changed into a co-operative and hard worker. But beyond that, he became a dynamic leader in the Christian Union. He was no weakling, but a strong, tough lad. No one in the school could help but notice the change and Kevin made sure they knew why. He didn't need years of teaching to prepare him to tell what Jesus had done for him – and many young and older people in that school wanted to hear what he had to say. This is the pattern of the New Testament, for the disciples of Jesus too learnt through mission, through testifying to what they had seen and heard and by living out the truth of which they spoke.

Misunderstandings

Christian young people do have hope, but what about the vast majority in our schools who are not Christians, who rarely enter a church and know little if anything of the gospel? Older people sometimes find it impossible to understand the young. Misunderstanding leads to fear and hostility. A typical reaction is reflected in this overheard snippet of conversation between two older ladies:

'They stand around by the shops and won't move out of your way . . . It can be quite frightening.'

'And they can be so rude.'

'I think they ought to bring back corporal punishment in schools . . .'

A group of teenagers standing at a street corner or in a school playground can seem threatening, but it is their individual vulnerability which makes them need the security of their group. The apparent hostility is usually just a stance which won't lead to much action. We should have learnt by now – after all, for thousands of years adults have complained that never before were teenagers so rude and badly behaved! In 300 BC Aristotle wrote: 'When I look at the younger generation I despair of the future of civilisation.' More than 1,500 years later in AD 1274 Peter the Monk wrote: 'The world is passing through troublesome times. The young people of today think of nothing but themselves. They have no reverence for parents or old age. They are impatient of all restraint. They talk as if they know everything, and what passes for wisdom with us is foolishness to them. As for the girls, they are immodest and unwomanly in speech, behaviour and dress.'

Perhaps neither adults nor teenagers have changed much over the centuries! But it is all too easy to believe a caricature about teenagers. In doing so we devalue them, treating them as an anonymous group rather than as individual human beings with their own personalities, talents, fears and aspirations.

Today, however, there is often more to a teenager's hostility than an adolescent simply trying to establish himself in the adult world. Teenagers have good reason to feel aggressive. The adults of their time have created a world of uncertainty, a world in which there is little personal, family, national or international security. No wonder they feel lost and betrayed. The very least we can do is to have compassion on them, try to understand their hurts and seek in every way to bring the healing which only Jesus can give.

Uncertainties

In an inner-city school in London a teacher asked a class of twelve- and thirteen-year-olds to recall any experiences of care they had received from someone else. After some hard thinking, one boy told the class of one time he remembered when he felt his mother had shown care towards him. He had hurt himself and as a result had been taken to the local hospital's casualty department. His father was called to the hospital to wait with him and then took him home. When they arrived, his father began to hit him repeatedly as a punishment for wasting his time over so small an injury. The boy's mother stubbed her cigarette on her husband's bare arms in an attempt to stop him beating their son. The boy told this story to his class perfectly seriously, as the one example he could remember of experiencing care from someone else. His classmates didn't show a flicker of surprise or disbelief. This was quite normal in their world. Many teenagers in our schools are not certain if they are loved, even by their parents.

In almost every class in every secondary school there are almost certainly a good number of children from broken homes. In an RE class discussion some twelve-year-olds were talking about letters they had received in the last few days. One boy put up his hand to say that he had just had a letter to say his father was getting married again; another lad told the class that he had recently received an invitation to his dad's wedding. They were both as matter-of-fact as if they were talking about letters from pen-friends. Any bitterness or confusion over the subject was well-hidden. Society seems to believe that if it says loud enough and long enough that marriage breakdown is acceptable, then the painful consequences will eventually go away. Sadly, many young people bury their hurt and their divided loyalties because this seems the right thing to do and because many of them with staggering generosity want to forgive their parents and not disturb them further by expressing their own grief or anger.

Often a teenager whose parents have split up feels a deep sense of outrage. If there is no outlet for this he or she may become extremely frustrated and bitter against both individuals and society. Jill, for example, was about fifteen, although she seemed older on first meeting her. People expected her to be more mature than she was and then were surprised when her moods and behaviour seemed irrational. One moment she wanted to be at the forefront of things; the next she wanted to hide. Talking with her revealed a painful background. Her parents had made friends with another couple. Then Jill's father had walked out on the family. The husband from the other couple had moved in with Jill's mother, bringing with him his two small children. His wife had set up home with Jill's father. Jill inevitably felt betrayed by all of them. She wanted to love her mother, but couldn't understand why she had brought these outsiders into their home. In particular she couldn't cope with the two young children who were very noisy and demanding, interrupting her concentration on her O-level work. Her mother's loyalties were divided between her boyfriend, his children and her own daughter and consequently she gave Jill little support. When asked how she felt about her father who had left them, Jill's reaction was abrasive: 'My father – I can't stand him!'

Jill is in some ways one of the lucky ones. She found a caring Christian teacher in her school who was prepared to listen to her, to be patient when she was truculent, and to point her towards Jesus Christ. She found friends in a local church and lively Christian fellowship. Most in Jill's situation have to cope alone. With such instability in our nation's home life, who can wonder at the insecurity of so many young people? What hope is there for them to establish loving, secure relationships for the next generation? How can they decide what is right or wrong, and how can we lead them to a God we rightly call 'Father'?

If the present is uncertain, the future is even more so. Every day the media bombards us with news of unemployment. Radio 1 gives friendly advice; BBC Nine O'Clock News states the cold facts. The message is all the same for the teenager: there is little chance of a job when you leave school. That means no money for the things you also couldn't afford with pocket money, no independence from parents. After years of being told that they are the bright ones and on target for good exam results, the clever ones discover that O- and A-level passes don't guarantee their future. Those who are not so successful academically begin to feel there is not much point in trying. 'Why bother to work when there are no jobs?' is their feeling.

It was sad to meet an unemployed boy at an inter-school meeting for Christian pupils. Throughout secondary school he had set his hopes on training as a mechanic. He had left school a few months earlier to discover there were no jobs for young trainees in his area. It really wasn't a question of trying harder to find a job – there simply were none. Even though most of the people at the meeting were several years younger than him, he had wanted to come; partly because he had nothing else to do and partly because he had come to meetings like this when he was a pupil and the world of school at least offered some security. At a time when teenagers should be looking forward to life with confidence, they are instead faced with harsh, unwelcome realities which make them want to give up on life before they have really begun.

A Glimmer of Light

In this darkness of moral confusion, unemployment and threat of nuclear conflict there is a glimmer of light. Where there is despair and confusion, people look for comfort and a leader. Where society provides no absolutes, people search to discover a basis for right and wrong. Where life seems pointless, people look for meaning. Amongst these thousands of young people who come together each day in our schools, there is hope. Many of them want to find answers to life and find out why the world seems to be going so badly wrong. They are at a time of life when experiences are fresh, topical issues new, and they won't be fobbed off with easy answers. They haven't had time to become apathetic and they want to know the truth. This is the church's opportunity. Many young people are ready to listen. Other groups in society are prepared to put a great deal of energy, time and money into communicating their respective messages. But it is often the wrong answer, couched in attractive tones which deceive the teenager. We Christians have sometimes been lacking in compassion and have been reticent in speaking out the truth of Jesus Christ. Yet at a time when there is confusion and young people long for a guide, we fail to point them to the one leader who won't let them down.

Young Christians committed to the lordship of Christ are like the leaven in the lump of dough. Through the life-giving work of the Holy Spirit and a renewed vision of what God wants to do in this suffering section of our society, through the genuine support of the rest of the Body of Christ, that leaven can begin to make its influence felt.

2

Pressures

Isolation

Thirty years ago a school of seven or eight hundred seemed large. Today in our huge machine-like schools, up to 2,000 young people struggle to find a sense of personal identity. They are unlikely to know the rest of the people in their year, let alone in the rest of the school. And it is small hope that all the teachers will know who your child is. Standing in a corridor at breaktime, the teacher on duty will probably see only a few familiar faces. Apart from the pupils and teachers, the school community includes, among others, administrators, secretaries, laboratory technicians, audio-visual and resources staff, a caterer, cooks, a librarian, a caretaker and peripatetic music teachers. Even teachers probably won't know all the other staff members personally.

Unlike the primary school where most children – their personalities, abilities, problems and home backgrounds – are likely to be well-known, it is easy for the individual teenager in secondary school to be just another face, another name on the register. Few schools have halls big enough for everyone to meet together at one time and this is just one more thing that makes it difficult to engender a sense of community.

It is not surprising that for many young people this is, after the protective world of the primary school, a daunting environment in which to live and work. For many, albeit unconsciously, it can lead to loneliness and a loss of their sense of individual worth. If a teenager is an extrovert or a leader then he or she can fight to be seen and heard; but if he or she is quiet and retiring it is easy to pass through school unnoticed, particularly if he or she is remarkable neither for failing nor succeeding academically.

Many young Christians at school do seem to work at keeping a low profile. Their fear of rejection keeps them from saying too much. Lunches eaten in a corner with a friend away from everyone else, heads down during lessons make the day pass quickly. The opposite temptation for Christians is to want to be noticed and accepted so desperately that personal beliefs and principles are played down or not mentioned so that it is possible to become one of the crowd. Some, of course, do have the confidence and courage to be truly themselves in standing up for their beliefs and make friends happily with both Christians and non-Christians.

Whatever his or her personality, at least the Christian can have a fundamental sense of his or her worth in Jesus Christ. For the non-Christian it is much harder. In every class there always seems to be at least one reject, the butt for everyone's teasing, the person who is always left to make his way to the next class alone. Even amongst those who are apparently successful socially and academically, a confident facade often conceals a deep sense of loneliness. Our individualistic society appears not to like those who make themselves vulnerable and admit their doubts, fears and problems. So people keep quiet and hide their worries behind a cheerful exterior.

In this depersonalised world one of the ways in which believers can witness is by trying at every opportunity to give worth and dignity to their fellow members of the community. This might mean making a point of befriending the rejects. It may mean not rushing off at breaktime to be with special friends, but waiting to talk with the lonely ones. It may mean speaking up in defence of those who have become too demoralised or who are too afraid to defend themselves. In general terms it will mean not thinking only of self, but taking time to put others first, doing a good turn without expecting to be paid back and making time to listen. Above all Christians in school can show by the way they relate to one another that the individual matters and is important to God.

A girl from a Gloucestershire school provided this lovely example of witness to Christ's life-changing power through her caring action as well as her words of testimony. After a session in the school Christian Union on the subject of witness, she said, 'But I can never think of the words to say in time.' Her Christian friends joined in with: 'Yes, but whenever people have problems, whether or not they are Christians, they come and talk to you because they know you will listen.' The individual is of infinite worth to God, and young Christians can begin to show this as they serve fellow believers and non-Christians alike in an attitude of self-forgetfulness. In doing so, both they and others will begin to discover their own self-worth.

Materialism

The struggle for personal identity has given birth to the 'Me-generation'. In a society which makes the individual feel insignificant and powerless, young people have searched for a culture that will give them a sense of worth. 'If no one else is going to look after me, then I will; and I will survive whatever the cost to anyone else,' is the attitude. Selfishness breeds selfishness.

Spiritual reality may not appeal to most teenagers, but the material world certainly does. Ownership is a powerful way of establishing your identity and popularity with peers. We live in an excessively rich period in material terms, in spite of unemployment. In one village primary school assembly, two hundred children were asked if any of them had visited Disneyland in the USA. Twelve children put their hands up. Almost all had been abroad for holidays. On a visit to a secondary school, I asked several classes of thirteen-year-olds how many of them had their own computer at home. At least half of the members of most classes had one.

Twenty-year-olds of the anti-establishment, freedom-loving sixties are now the respectable middle-aged parents of today's teenagers. For many of them security is now found in the best house, car, video or microwave oven they can afford. The present generation of young people is eagerly following their example.

A week's mission in one school revealed a community which seemed almost totally devoid of spiritual awareness. As far as pupils were concerned, the reason for coming to school was the hope of an eventual 'good job with lots of money'. It wasn't that the young people were unhelpfully argumentative or hostile – it would have been easier if they were. For the most part, they simply weren't bothered about Christianity. Their response seemed to be a uniform, 'You believe in God? – So what?' 'Isn't there more to life?' they were asked. Polite, intelligent sixth-formers replied, 'If being a Christian helps you, fine'; but for them, it was obvious that everyone must look after Number One – and a good job, a car, a house, plenty of money and a husband or wife were the only symbols of success that they were looking for.

Apart from this frightening lack of imagination into which Satan has trapped so many young people, one of his most effective tricks is to persuade people that they are worth only what they own. They need the power and life of Jesus to break out of this, and there are a few who are making this happy discovery.

For young Christians at school, this is an important area of witness. Teenagers need to know that they have worth not because of what they own or even because of their abilities, but because of the infinite value God has placed on them. However important a person may or may not seem, each one has indescribable worth because he or she is created in the image of God and because God in Jesus Christ gave his life for them. Christians in school can bring this message of security and freedom to their non-Christian friends by their own attitudes to what others may or may not own and by their attitudes to their own belongings and the generosity and unselfishness with which they share them. Non-Christian teenagers idolise material things because they give identity and security; and because fundamentally they unconsciously believe only in the reality of this world, rather than in the reality of eternity. When young Christians show that they are not dependent on, dominated by or impressed by 'things', not only do they affirm the individual's intrinsic worth, they also implicitly suggest that there is more to life than just this temporal world with its belongings.

Many young Christians are not even aware of this subtle challenge to their faith. They need the help and teaching of older members of the church to understand and follow Christ's standards in this area. For many adults this will mean that first of all they need to change, before they can challenge the young with integrity.

Fashion

The search for identity continues in two areas central to youth culture: dress and music. Often adults are afraid of young people simply because they look different. A garishly dressed teenager walking down the road or standing belligerently in the middle of the pavement might tempt them to cross the road nervously and to mutter to their companion disapprovingly. As Christians God calls us to go beyond our first superficial reaction and to look at the real person beneath the make-up and hairstyle.

Teenagers have long sought to establish their own identity by the clothes they wear, be it the teddy-boy image of the fifties or the mini-skirt and winkle-pickers of the sixties. In the early eighties the punks' clashing colours, hard lines and disfigurement of hair and face cocked a snook at authority, pointed to a rejection of adult values and a disenchantment with the society they have inherited. Teenage fashion, even in its gentler forms, has increasingly become a matter of playing a part. In a world which seems meaningless, in which the reality is sometimes too awful to contemplate, escape into fantasy is tempting. In a lonely world clothes are also the badge which guarantees acceptance in a group; and teenagers are not alone in this – adults too have plenty of group rules for dress.

Whilst there are un-Christian undertones in some current trends of fashion, much is also just good fun. Young Christians won't help their witness to their peers by unattractive dowdiness. The important thing is that young Christians don't live as if outward appearance was all that mattered; but that does not mean that they can't be fashionable. They need to use their God-given imaginations to dress in a way that brings attractive colour and life to a dull world; dress which makes others feel at ease rather than threatened, and dress which points to the one who rules in their lives – the God who brings originality and harmony to our world.

Music

The music of the young, like their fashions can be shocking. Much of it aims to be so. Like dress, it too can express outrage at a world in pain, laughing at those things which we can no longer cry about; and, like fashion, much is simply an escape into fantasy. It has become a contentious issue for Christians.

Certainly the way in which music dominates the lives of some teenagers seems unhealthy. The powerful influence of rock musicians is awesome. Young people absorb their style – morals, language, attitudes to authority – without being aware of what is happening. We must not, however, over-react. We are in the notoriously difficult area of personal taste. Beethoven's contemporaries thought he was mad when he wrote his seventh symphony because of the key changes in the work and even in the relatively tame area of church music the introduction of the organ in the nineteenth century caused an outcry amongst those who preferred the bass-viol, serpent and clarinet. Closer home, the music of Mr. Sankey's hymns only reflected the popular music of the day and General Booth's Salvation Army music was in the style of the working-class music hall. We need to be careful not to turn our private prejudices into biblical principles.

A Christian boy at a young people's weekend talked about the struggle he was having with rock music. Was it right to listen to it? He loved the music but couldn't believe that it was all right for a Christian. The real problem was that he wanted an easy, blanket answer: either it was all wrong or he could listen to anything he liked.

He was, in fact, facing the problem that Christians face in many areas of life, whether it be music, TV, politics or even shopping: how to be discerning. Like all those things, rock music is a mixed bag. The apostle Paul tells us to concentrate on things which are true, noble, right, pure, lovely and admirable (Philippians 4:8). But they are not necessarily things which are comfortable. You can no more say that all rock music is bad than say that all TV is unacceptable. Much certainly is – but not all.

So what should he do? Maybe for him at that stage the whole issue had become such a big thing that it was right to put it on one side for a while until he got things in proportion. But it would have been a shame if he had simply retreated into a world where his renewed mind lay dormant and he never developed discernment. The fact is that all of us need to bring our Christian minds to the music we enjoy; whether it be classical, Hollywood romanticism or contemporary rock, each style has its own wheat and tares. Mature Christians grow from young Christians who have learnt to think biblically and take responsibility for their actions under the lordship of Christ.

The world of music is a huge part of youth culture and the issue is much bigger than the music itself. It brings with it a whole sub-culture – concerts, videos, dress and lifestyle. For teenage Christians whose friends are totally involved in all of this, it is very difficult to stand on the outside and even more difficult to tread carefully through this jungle avoiding the traps.

Sex

John is a recently converted seventeen-year-old. His father has just asked him if he is sleeping with his girlfriend yet. He is now old enough to do so. John is only just beginning to understand Christian teaching – and he has to stand alone for his principles. But what hope for the non-Christian teenager?

Upside down sexual morality is one of many confusing and hurtful aspects of today's pagan society. Certainly it is one of the areas where young Christians need to make a clear stand for Jesus Christ, not in a judgemental way but to show that God's way is the best and most satisfying.

It is hardly surprising that many young people have a distorted view of God's precious gift of sex. Their parents have set a poor example. Kate, for example, a cheerful fourteen-year-old who knows how to take care of herself in a tough world and isn't always easy on her teachers, talked in matter-of-fact tones about her mum's latest boyfriend who was living with them. She had no idea of the enormity of the change in society that her casual attitude towards him represented. Television has compounded the picture. Again and again, throughout an evening's viewing it is suggested that it is quite normal to sleep with a boy or girlfriend and that is, after all, what the friendship is all about.

Many TV situation comedies depict broken homes as the norm.

All teenagers in school are aware that many of their friends' parents have split up or have a boy or girlfriend. This is just an everyday fact of life. With this adult example to follow, who can blame teenagers for wanting to prove their maturity and increase their prestige by being amongst the first to sleep with their partner? In school it is the teenagers who are in the majority; they talk openly and emphatically and it is the ethos they create that is important. If you are a member of that community, it is very hard not to be influenced in some way, even if it is only in no longer being shocked. It is almost impossible for the non-Christian teenager to find a way through the maze of moral rights and wrongs; for the Christian young person there is a way, but it's hard.

Adult members of the Christian community don't always quite understand or believe how difficult it can be for young people to witness for Christ in this area. For the teenage boy, in particular, there is tremendous pressure on him to prove his masculinity. To have slept with a girl is regarded as prestigious. It's not just a case of youthful sexual curiosity either. Society, through the media, suggests in a thousand ways that sleeping with your girl is acceptable and even admirable. The Christian girl who sticks to her principles is in danger of cruel teasing and accusations of being a prude. Amongst some girls, taking the pill has become a kind of status symbol. Of course, some of the talk is just youthful boasting, but we are blind if we don't see that for many teenagers, sexual activity is the norm in the relationship of boy and girlfriend.

In the middle of a great tide of public opinion that tells us that sex outside of marriage is all right and that if you become pregnant when you are only fifteen it's a pity, but just one of those things, young Christians are understandably confused and genuinely begin to think that maybe it is all right after all, especially if you love each other. Older Christians, they say, just don't understand the way the world is, and young Christians don't want to be thought behind the times any more than other young people do.

A 'Relationships' session in a weekend away with the young people from a Baptist church revealed the real confusion that

27

some Christian teenagers feel. Lorraine, a likeable, outgoing girl, was a new Christian who had had little teaching. She listened attentively as it was carefully explained how the Bible taught that sex was intended for marriage alone. Lorraine couldn't wait for the question time to arrive; she interrupted the talk with: 'Are you honestly saying that it's wrong to sleep with your boyfriend? As you've been talking my thoughts have been going round and round . . . I need some time to think about this . . .' Her face showed the inward struggle she was going through. This Christian girl had never been exposed to biblical teaching on this subject before and what she heard was painfully turning her thinking right way up. Lorraine was in no way an obvious rebel; she was down-to-earth, friendly and normal. Her problem was only that no one had ever told her in an uncompromising way what God wanted of her in the area of sex and relationships.

Another schoolgirl in the same group who was to be baptised the following weekend asked: 'Is it all right for Christians to take the pill?'

The leader clarified: 'Do you mean if someone is married?'

'No . . . any time.'

'Why would a Christian want to take the pill?' the leader probed. The girl looked embarrassed. This young Christian had absorbed the attitude of her non-Christian peers, that it is better to be safe than sorry, not seeing that to take the pill as an unmarried girl was to put herself in the way of temptation and was a compromise in her thinking.

This same group wanted to know whether it was wrong to 'go out' with a non-Christian. Some of the youth leaders of this group had discussed the matter already and felt that it was too great a burden to place on young Christians to say that they shouldn't have a non-Christian girl or boyfriend, in spite of the fact that biblical teaching, not to mention common sense, suggests that a close personal relationship between a Christian and a non-Christian isn't wise. They felt that present day trends should be taken into account and that the situation had changed. The devil is very subtle.

In a similar discussion with a Brethren youth fellowship where the majority were Christians, a non-Christian boy spoke up, quite unabashed: 'I'm not a Christian and it doesn't seem to make any difference to our relationship, does it Jane?' His Christian girlfriend sat in silence throughout the discussion.

It's easy to be disapproving of the young, yet we cannot expect them to give a clear witness in this area unless we are also prepared to help them discover and apply the guidelines found in the Bible. It also helps us to understand the tensions which exist for teenagers, although it doesn't solve them, if we remember that in past centuries physical maturity came later, but marriage came earlier. Today physical maturity arrives early yet education and financial dependence means that marriage is delayed.

What the media don't tell people about is the burden of guilt that follows sexual sin. For many it is quickly suppressed; for others it eats away inside them for years with no outlet or solution. Many sincere and well-meaning non-Christians refuse to recognise sin; the emphasis is rather that a person has a problem and needs help. One radio 'phone-in programme expert even told a caller, troubled by sexual sin and not being able to change, to stop worrying – he didn't need to change or feel guilty because he was doing nothing wrong. Such 'compassion' doesn't help individuals with their problems. Relief from guilt can only come when the person is helped to see that he has broken God's law and that there is a remedy in Jesus Christ.

Just as unhelpful, however, can be the unsympathetic reaction of some Christians. Christine, for example, is a seventeen-year-old who made a somewhat shaky beginning to her Christian life. She found it particularly hard to stand out from the crowd and tended to blend, chameleon-style, with whichever group she was with. There was, however, no doubt about the intensity of guilt and sorrow she felt after having slept with her boyfriend. So painful was the memory, she found it difficult to speak about; but almost more distressing to her was the reaction of her church youth leaders when, in attempting to put things right, she confessed to them what she had done, only to find she was met with obvious suspicion. She went away feeling that because of her confession, her testimony to faith in Christ was held in doubt. Yet Christians should be the last to be shocked, knowing so much more clearly than others what is in the heart of man.

The world in particular, but also some parts of the church, finds it difficult to understand that the sin and the sinner are separate. Whilst the sin needs condemnation, the sinner needs compassion, forgiveness and restoration. This is, after all, the pattern that Jesus set in his treatment of the woman taken in adultery. The world wants easy love and compassion; the church turns people away by seeming to offer only condemnation. In the hopeless tangle that the twentieth century has got itself into, along with its young, the good news of Jesus Christ brings hope and offers the only true solution.

Sex Education is included in the curriculum of most schools. It might be a subject in its own right or covered in Health Education or Biology or Religious Education. It has been the subject of considerable debate amongst parents and teachers. It is a fact that many parents find it difficult to talk openly and honestly with their children about sex. On balance, it would seem better that teenagers receive at least some factual teaching on the subject rather than the garbled and inaccurate information they may pick up anyway from fellow teenagers. For Christian parents it can be a difficult issue. The teacher for the subject will almost certainly not be a Christian and will not necessarily present a view which agrees with biblical teaching. Many teachers, as people in society generally, have no qualms about living with their boy or girlfriend outside of marriage. Few teachers would be irresponsible enough to emphasise their personal views in this area, but nevertheless, their prejudices and foundations for living are bound to be communicated in some ways.

One Christian teacher who was given the task of talking about sex with some senior girls in her school, made it clear that its place was within marriage. Some of the girls protested at this 'biased' view; they wanted to hear the other side of the story. What they expected to hear was that if you intended sleeping with your boyfriend, you should make sure you have adequate contraceptive protection.

An ambivalent view of sex is often taught in the classroom. It seems to have become a virtue in recent years, even amongst some Christian adults, to give no clear guidelines for right and wrong. Teenagers are taught the biological facts, what to do to prevent unwanted pregnancy and about the dangers of 'sleeping around'. Many teachers feel that young people should then be left to make up their own minds as a part of growing up is learning to make your own decisions. Whilst this may be true in some areas, in this particular one adults are often abdicating their own responsibilities to the young. God has given guidelines for the happiness and well-being of mankind. We ignore them at great cost. Unfortunately much of the cost is being borne by the young. The mistakes our society freely allows them to make for the sake of their 'maturity' can't be put right in a lifetime, but will leave permanent physical, emotional, psychological and spiritual scars.

One of the most harmful things which has been taught in the classroom by implication and confirmed through television and magazines is that sex is a separate issue from relationships. Teenagers have not learnt that the context for sex is only the very special relationship between one man and one woman in marriage; and that within marriage it expresses and cements the unity that already exists in every other area of their friendship. Instead of the upbuilding, security-providing gift that God intended it to be, so that a man and a woman could demonstrate their love and desire to give to one another, modern man has abused sex and turned it into an idol which threatens to destroy individual happiness and security.

On the brighter side, there is a growing sense amongst some teenagers that you should work out your own principles and then stick to them. Girls are becoming more outspoken in saying they have decided not to sleep with their boyfriend and will keep sex for marriage. The problem with this is that it confirms the secular view that says you can do whatever you like; there is still no basis for right and wrong. This, however, does make it easier for young Christians to say clearly what they believe.

Often Christian teenagers, trying to survive in a tough world, take the line of quiet resistance. They keep silent in conversations, passively condoning an unbiblical view of sexual morality; they smile politely in response to an unsavoury joke which devalues sex. Instead they need to speak out – not because it's their personal view, but because there is a God who is sovereign and he has given rules for living which bring happiness and wholeness rather than sadness and death. Unlike their classmates they will not be speaking on their own authority. They need to have the inner conviction that their God does exist, that he is right and that his word is truth. Somehow the church must communicate this confidence in our God to the younger members of the Body of Christ.

It was moving to hear a Christian girl of about eighteen speaking out on the subject in a mid-evening TV programme recently. It was a live discussion about the generation gap in families and took place in front of a studio audience. The issue of sexual morality was raised. In sharp contrast to the vague, 'do-as-you-think-right' answers of other participants, this girl told the audience very clearly that because she was a Christian and based her life on the Bible, she believed that the only place for sex was within marriage. In spite of her youthfulness and inexperience, there was a conviction and strength about her which in the close-up world of television marked her out from the other participants. Her comment was one of the few in the programme which raised serious debate.

Those at school may feel that, alone, they can't make much difference to what their non-Christian friends think or do. But when a Christian speaks out then perhaps just one other person is given the courage to stick to what he or she knows is right. Whilst there are those who will mock or sneer, there are many more who will listen and watch without comment and be quietly impressed. Years later they may remember and turn to Christ.

Maybe Christian young people need to set a new trend and start showing that life can be just as much fun for a mixed group of friends as the obligatory girl/boy friendship. One problem of today is that a simple, uncomplicated friendship between a boy and a girl is almost impossible; there always have to be overtones of 'going out', which is often a euphemism for too much physical involvement. Everyone knows that at this stage it is unlikely that 'going out' will lead to marriage, so why get so involved in the first place? If there are a number of Christians in school, this shouldn't lead to loneliness; instead it could be an opportunity to show non-Christians how good God-centred friendships are.

One youth group talking about the pressure to have a boy or girlfriend, pointed out that whilst they were able to accept the sense of this argument, it still wasn't easy when you were invited, for example, to a friend's party. Socially, girls are expected to have an escort and would feel out of things without one. This group had found a solution to the problem. The boys offered to accompany any of the girls who were invited to an event; they would go together simply as friends with no strings attached. Not only did this solve the problem of social etiquette, it also meant that the two Christians would be able to support each other in their witness amongst their non-Christian friends.

This topsy-turvy battlefield of sexual morality confronts Christian teenagers in one way or another every day as they go into school. Adults rarely have the opportunity to enter the world of teenage conversation. Christian young people do. Through them God's light can be brought to those who are lost. But in order for this to happen young Christians need to be equipped with strong biblical teaching; they need to know that they are not standing alone; and they need to be challenged to speak out against wrong and demonstrate positively a better way.

Media

All the struggles of being a young Christian in the midst of a distinctly non-Christian youth culture are intensified by the media. Advertising plays unashamedly on people's desire for material wealth and subtly encourages contempt for those who own little. One recent cancer research advertisement appealing for funds reads: 'Sooner or later we will find a cure for cancer. With your help it will be sooner', illustrating the pride of this generation which believes that provided it has the money it can do anything. Magazines affirm that physical appearance and successful relationships with the opposite sex are the most important aspects of our lives.

The average daily TV viewing time per person is three hours per day; for many young people it will be much more. Quietly and insidiously television works away telling young people that frequent drinking, sleeping with your girlfriend, sick jokes, expensive clothes and lifestyle are all normal and highly desirable. In addition to this, violence and the overthrow of authority are relished. They have become entertainment. Video nasties, easily available, corrupt the minds of the very young: some research has estimated that one third of children have seen one by the time they are eight years old. The teenager changes TV channel from violent fiction to factual war pictures of the dead and dying. We are bombarded with cruelty and bloodshed and in the comfort of the family living room, fiction and reality are distanced and merge. Our senses have become so dulled that it is hard to respond adequately when we hear of yet another murder in Northern Ireland.

This is the background against which young Christians are growing up – a society which has rejected the authority of God but has found nothing to put in its place. Society tells teenagers through its materialism, fashion, music, television, advertising and magazines: 'It's your life, not God's. Do what you like.' As a result people struggle to live their lives, realising too late that their so-called freedom imprisons many others.

Authority

Against the background of these pressures, there has been a steady decrease in respect for authority, law and order over the last few years. Not surprisingly this is reflected in the classroom. School discipline has become a contentious issue. Teachers have frequently received a bad press with easy accusations of incompetence. But they have a tough job. They are made the scapegoat for a society that wants them to impose the behaviour patterns and discipline which it has failed to provide.

As a young teacher I remember being confronted by an unruly all-boys fourth-year class. I was warned that they had 'destroyed' their last English teacher, who had left the school after a nervous breakdown. It felt a bit like being thrown to the lions! In one of the first lessons one of the boys asked gleefully: 'You know what we did to Mr. Green, don't you, Miss?' Those lads had a real sense of group power that was quite frightening. They were totally devoid of any conventional respect for the teacher. It is only fair to say that no one had ever shown much respect for them either; at school, on the street and at home they were at the bottom of the ladder.

Another teacher tells of the time when, during a lesson, she was telling off a teenage lad at the front of her classroom whilst the rest of the class was working. Without warning the boy took out a knife. At the same time two of his friends from the class came up and pinned her against the blackboard, whilst the boy with the knife waved it threateningly in front of the teacher. Inwardly she prayed. Just at that moment the headmaster's voice was heard in the corridor outside. As the door handle turned the boy's knife was put away and by the time the headmaster had opened the door, all appeared perfectly normal – three boys talking to the teacher whilst the rest of the class was working.

These examples may be extreme cases, but they serve to illustrate that there is no longer the traditional respect for authority figures that once existed. For the Christian teenager it is difficult not to pick up the attitudes of fellow classmates to authority and this in turn can affect attitudes to work. It is all very well knowing with your head that the Bible commands respect for those with authority and teaches that all work should be done as well as possible because it is for the honour of God, but it is not so easy to put into practice in a classroom with twenty-nine other people who have a different basis for living.

One of the factors we often forget when thinking about disruptive pupils is that many of them who are at present in the fourth and fifth years of secondary school wouldn't have been there at all a few years ago. It may well be that they shouldn't be there today. School is inappropriate to the needs of many teenagers. The narrow emphasis on examination success which our education system has from fourteen years upwards means that many who are not academically successful are daily reminded of their 'failure'. They have other skills and areas of their lives in which they can succeed, but at present our school system doesn't provide for their development.

Smoking behind the bike sheds, smuggling a can of beer into school for a covert drink between lessons and, more recently, glue-sniffing are all well-tried methods of rebelling against authority and proving to the world that you are growing up. The majority of young people are able to avoid these pitfalls or at least learn quickly after one or two mistakes. The ones who are most vulnerable are those who feel themselves to be on the edges of the community; those who are not seen to be successful – whether it be academically, in their personalities, in sport or because of family background. Often the regular smoking gang are a small group of young people who have a very special need of being valued; the secret glue-sniffers may seem to be just

35

wayward kids out for a laugh, but the habit often hides a gulf of emptiness and the excitement of a fix provides a welcome escape from hard reality. These are the victims of our society who dig their own graves.

From the safety of churches and youth fellowships, from the warmth and security of Christian families, this is the world into which Christians are sent unprepared and ill-equipped. Their task isn't easy. The Bible doesn't promise that it will be. Is there still a place for God in school?

3

A place for God?

Religious Education and the School Curriculum

Jenny was depressed, confused and considering whether in all honesty she could continue as a Christian. An intelligent, mischievous seventeen-year-old, she had seemed back in the summer at a sixth-form Bible study week, to be one of the most mature and enthusiastic Christians in the group.

The problem was A-level Religious Education. Her class had been studying the life of David in the Old Testament. The teacher had said that David's life was not based on his concern for God at all, but was instead entirely politically motivated – he just used God. Her teacher argued so convincingly, that Jenny began to wonder if this was true for other great heroes of the Old Testament too. Perhaps all the great holy men of the past that she had believed in and learnt from were, in fact, motivated by self-interest; perhaps even Jesus himself was only using God. With no one else in the class having a strong, personal faith to back her up, Jenny was left alone to argue her case and began to feel all that she had based her life on was crumbling. Perhaps the 'evangelical' view was wrong, based on false arguments for its own ends.

At the other end of the school age bracket, an eight-year-old boy came home from school one day and disturbed his Christian parents by asking, 'You can't know for certain you are going to heaven, can you?' A teacher had told his class that it wasn't possible to know for certain that you were going to heaven. This small boy, like many other children, automatically felt he should believe what the teacher said rather than what his parents had taught him. Teachers have a great deal of influence.

In all the debate about RE, perhaps the most worrying aspect is not simply the matter of content, but the implications that are made in the way it is taught. In matter-of-fact tones what is really a liberal view of the Bible is often communicated. The young Christian may not even notice and the non-Christian just accepts whatever is taught because the teacher is the authority on the subject. Even if the Christian does notice, when, for example, the miracles or the resurrection are explained away as symbols rather than hard fact, it is difficult to be brave enough to speak up for the truth. The teacher has a great deal more theological knowledge than his pupils and he has the prestige of being the professional. In addition there are twenty-nine other people in the classroom who would think one stupid for caring about it.

It is not that teachers intentionally try to put forward their own views at the expense of others; but humanly speaking it is almost impossible to present with conviction the evidence for the resurrection if you don't believe it yourself. Christian young people can at least go home or to their churches and talk through these issues and hear the other side of the story; young people with no church background just accept what is taught. Gradually God is diminished to man's size whilst, paradoxically, man is elevated to become a god in his own right.

Some Christian parents are concerned that RE in many schools includes learning about other religions alongside Christianity. Most RE teachers, however, would see their function as not to call pupils to belief in any one particular faith, but rather to give education about religion – its development throughout history and present day religions of the world. Some syllabuses also include moral education and at the very least, for all its failings, RE is the one subject on the school curriculum that clearly points to a spiritual dimension in life. To say that the facts about the Hindu faith shouldn't be taught is as illogical as saying that American history or the geography of India shouldn't have a place in the classroom. With so many people of different ethnic backgrounds with a variety of faiths moving into Britain, it is important that young people should be helped to understand the basis of culture and life of other races and nationalities. One great danger, however, is the subtle implication that there is no absolute truth about God.

Although it is legitimate to teach the facts about other

religions, there is a clear case for protest if this is done at the expense of teaching about Christianity and the Bible. The whole of western society is founded on its Christian heritage – arts, history, values and laws. Without a clear understanding of the Christian faith and a basic knowledge of the Bible, a young person's understanding of our society and culture will be severely limited. Much literature, history, music and art is incomprehensible without considerable knowledge of the Bible. For example, Milton's *Paradise Lost* cannot be properly understood without knowledge of the biblical material it uses; the effects of the Reformation on the history of Europe and Britain cannot be understood without some understanding of the Christian faith.

Irrespective of the subject content, some people question whether RE should be on the school curriculum at all. This is perhaps a sad reflection of a society which only considers material things to be of value. It is also argued that religion is purely a personal matter and shouldn't take up time on the school timetable. This argument again suggests that there is no absolute truth about God – yet surely education should above all be concerned about the discovery of truth. It also suggests that people's private and public lives are separate. In the USA there is no teaching of RE in state schools because there is a separation of state and religion. This has helped to create an ethos which says that God is a personal matter and has nothing to do, for example, with politics or any other major area of life. This denies the Christian conviction that God is concerned about and involved in every area of life: belief in him affects both our private and public life and shapes our thinking on every issue.

Whilst in some schools RE is considered of equal importance to History or Geography, in many schools it has a very low status. There is perhaps only one RE specialist who has to cope with several non-specialist teachers, who have little training or personal motivation for teaching the subject, taking one or two periods per week. A typical example of this was a Physical Education teacher who had reluctantly agreed to teach some RE. He felt totally out of his depth, not because he was opposed to RE, but simply because he knew little about the subject and had no interest in 'religion'. In addition to this, there may be very limited resources for the development of the RE department so that it is impossible to afford new materials, filmstrips and books. If other staff members regard RE as the least important of subjects, then it will suffer most in the allocation of funds, periods per week, rooms and staffing. Lack of resources and good teaching staff for the first two years of secondary school mean that it is difficult for the head of RE to make the subject lively and interesting for pupils. This results in fewer opting for RE examination courses. In many teachers' eyes the importance of a subject depends on its examination successes. In RE it's a vicious circle; as a result of meagre resources few opt for RE in the fourth year and as a result of that the headmaster reduces the resources that are available even further. RE teachers often have quite a struggle and not surprisingly many become resigned and demoralised.

If the headmaster doesn't believe in the importance of the subject, he may well not be too stringent in his selection and appointment of an RE specialist. Even though the teaching of RE is statutory, it is amazing how little of the subject can end up on the timetable. I remember being involved in a week of mission in one school where the one RE teacher seemed to have little interest in his own subject or in the views of the visitors who were taking some of his classes. He didn't even turn up to some of his lessons to introduce us to the class. Presumably, however outrageous our teaching he wouldn't have cared or noticed. In this school the only genuine RE slot on the timetable was in the third year. In first and second years it was submerged and diluted in Humanities and not surprisingly, in view of the small amount of time it was allowed and the low morale of the one specialist, very few young people opted to take an O-level or CSE course in the fourth and fifth years. The teenagers in this school, as in many others, seemed to feel that the subject was pointless and a waste of time.

When RE is reduced in this way, it does untold damage. For many young people, RE lessons are the only place that they will hear about God, the Bible and Christianity. If it is given little importance in the school curriculum and badly taught, then a generation of young people may leave school quite convinced that all religion, including Christianity, is boring and irrelevant. It just confirms what the media says about the church and religion: at best vicars are funny, but certainly their message isn't to be taken seriously.

In spite of the discouragements, there are many Christian RE teachers who are fighting hard to put the subject on a sound academic basis. Some have won back O- and A-level courses through prayerful dedication, enthusiasm and excellent teaching. Many have succeeded in recovering much needed prestige for the subject by creating exciting, biblically based syllabuses.

For many years RE has been a focus for Christian debate about education; as a subject it gives the most obvious opportunities for a biblical world view to be challenged or misrepresented. Consequently in many churches, young Christians have been alerted to possible areas of conflict and the most enthusiastic are ready to speak out for their beliefs. Yet whilst Christians have written and spoken much about miracles being dismissed in the classroom or the creation story being treated as myth, a silent revolution has been taking place in the curriculum which is much less of an obvious threat to Christian beliefs but is more sinister. Twenty or thirty years ago education – whatever the subject – had the fundamental premise that God existed, the Bible was truth, God's law was to be obeyed. Now all that has changed. Quietly God has been ousted and put on one side. God has become an irrelevance – believe in him if you like but that belief has nothing to do with the world of education. Academic study and discipline structures in schools now focus on man – his judgements, his problems, his achievements, his knowledge and his power.

Whilst the evolution/creation debate still rages amongst evangelicals it is not that much of an issue in the science classroom. God simply doesn't come into it. The theory of evolution is taught as though it were an irrefutable fact. Many Christian young people who are growing up in a society which accepts evolution, simply absorb the teaching and maintain an ambivalent view of God's part in the beginning of the world. The matter of greatest concern is not the various arguments in the creation/evolution debate, but the general acceptance that God no longer has a place in intelligent, serious discussion.

This man-centred attitude is an underlying element in other subjects too. The Humanities are often treated as one subject on

41

the timetable and can include a whole range of subjects which were formerly separate such as History, Geography, Religious Education, English and Social Sciences. Humanities, as the name suggests, concentrates on man: his efforts and achievements, individual and societal development. Events are seen as dependent on man's activity.

The school curriculum of today powerfully communicates to young people that God is not important (or interesting maybe!), that the Bible is irrelevant and that there is no absolute right or wrong. The Bible tells us that God is the source of all truth. If the educational establishments of the present dismiss God from the curriculum then, but for God's grace, the society of the future can only be founded on falsehood.

School Assembly

Britain is no longer a Christian society. Christians ought not therefore to be surprised when people do not live by Christian principles. When the 1944 Education Act, which at the time of writing is still the basis of our education system, was framed most people would have regarded themselves as Christians and would have seen Great Britain as a Christian country. But we now have a situation where it is claimed that there are more Muslims than Methodists and where only a small percentage of the population are regular church-goers. School assemblies highlight the problem. The 'daily act of worship' is still statutory and causes many a crisis of conscience amongst teachers who freely admit to having no Christian faith. For them to lead a religious assembly is to act a lie. The result of this unease, plus the lack of school halls big enough to hold large numbers of pupils, is that the law has been interpreted more and more liberally, so that few pupils now attend daily assemblies and the content of these will by no means always refer to God. In state schools where there is still a daily religious assembly teachers and pupils alike in many cases find it a distinctly uncomfortable experience. As few pupils would call themselves Christians, the whole procedure can become a gross act of hypocrisy, which is both tedious and embarrassing.

Many pupils have an automatic switch-off mechanism when it comes to assemblies. Their minds will be filled with last night's TV programmes or today's Maths test, whilst their bodies remain passive as the strange little rigmarole of a weakly sung hymn, a platitudinous homily and a nebulous prayer drift over them without meaning. After all, what has God to do with school? So well constructed are the defences that even if an assembly is lively and interesting, people are unlikely to notice.

Taking an assembly as a visitor in a school, can be a fairly awesome business. Several hundred pairs of teenage eyes watch and wait critically. If anything too directly challenging is said, they are joined by the cold stares of the teaching staff. Well-tried illustrations which usually evoke a response from teenagers, are received with restraint. No one is quite sure if you are allowed to laugh in assembly. On the occasions when there seems to be a genuine response of any sort, it is quickly swept away and forgotten as the ageing deputy head rises to his feet and, after politely thanking you, proceeds in angry tones to berate and threaten certain wayward pupils for yet more misdemeanours!

Some Christian teachers decide not to go to the school assembly, fearing that their Christian testimony may be identified with a dull, hypocritical ritual. School assemblies can be a disaster area for the Christian faith.

The official God-spot on the school timetable may be the only taste of 'Christianity' that some young people ever experience. It is hardly surprising that a good many of them decide that they don't want to enquire further. Some adults in the church are concerned that few schools now have a religious assembly, but we need to face the fact that we are living in a pagan society. Non-Christian headmasters and teachers cannot communicate a lively understanding of the Christian faith. The daily, empty ritual instead turns many people away from a real encounter with God.

If the daily, religious assembly does remain statutory, the one hope is that more and more Christians both from inside and outside of school will take the opportunity of leading them. Non-Christian staff are usually only too pleased if someone else is willing to take on this task. Christians can lead in the spirit of: 'This is what I believe. What do you think?' Many Christian teenagers are already taking up this challenge and regularly leading an assembly. They may not have the professional confidence of teachers, but at least they believe what they say and the reality of their faith shows. Some schools have got round the problem of assemblies by providing voluntary Christian assemblies. These give the opportunity for specifically Christian content and uninhibited, un-hypocritical worship for those who have chosen to come. At the present time the whole matter of Religious Education in schools and of statutory religious assemblies is under discussion and change may well be on the way. It is important that Christians should be involved in the debate.

The Occult

Many teenagers are looking for spiritual meaning in their lives and unaware of the good news of Jesus, turn to ouija boards and tarot cards as attractive and exciting playthings. But not for long.

Elaine came to her teacher shaking with fear. Usually the sort who means trouble in a lively third-year class, now she was vulnerable and too scared to care about showing it. Messing with spiritism isn't just for fun. For once the shutters were up and she looked out desperate for help. She agreed to pray with the teacher to God asking for his help and protection, intuitively sensing that he was good and more powerful than the forces of darkness she had met. Interestingly, a couple of days later, when her teacher asked her how she was, she seemed to have no recollection of their conversation or of praying together. Perhaps it was just that she was back to her normal self and wasn't prepared to admit any chinks in the armour. On the other hand she genuinely seemed surprised at the enquiry, so maybe it was simply that God had completely taken away any memories of a very frightening incident.

Fortunately there are comparatively few who become as deeply involved in spiritism as Elaine. For her the occult had always been much more than a game. Adults in her family had taught her to fear and believe in evil spirits and one of her close relatives was a medium. For most teenagers ouija boards and seances are fads which pass through school from time to time and have similar status to experiments with smoking behind the bike sheds. For a while they are exciting, but after two or three sessions it becomes perhaps too frightening or more likely too boring and it is forgotten. For some though, the consequences are serious. It may all start as a game, but gradually the teenager is drawn into belief, only to discover too late that the devil is a hard taskmaster.

Ruth spent most of a young people's houseparty in tears. It was hard to get her to speak, but when she finally agreed to chat with one of the leaders, she explained, between sobs, that she had been involved in a number of seances. Talking with her, it seemed extremely unlikely that she was 'possessed' as she feared. But she was still desperately afraid that Satan had some kind of long-term power over her as a result of the seances. She also felt extremely guilty, so much so that she couldn't believe that God would accept her. Ruth was fortunate in being befriended by young Christians in her school who were very sensible and patient with her. They brought her along to another Christian camp a few months later and eventually she was able to accept God's forgiveness and a much more peaceful girl emerged. In Ruth's case, seances were only part of her problem, but this example shows how apparently harmless involvement in such things can play havoc in the imaginations and lives of teenagers – creating fear and guilt, leaving awful memories which can torture them for years afterwards.

Just as serious are the unseen consequences which affect many young people who dabble in the occult unaware of its dangers. When little importance is attached to playing with tarot cards or a ouija board, young people can become resilient against all that is spiritual. God also becomes just a game. The media has much to answer for with its light treatment of the occult. Horoscopes have become a fun interlude in a serious news programme. Presented in an affable, jovial style, the whole subject is made to seem perfectly harmless. Teenagers at a school in Hull began to experiment with a ouija board after seeing one used in a popular television series. Fortunately, in this case, a Christian teacher in their school discovered what they were doing and was able to explain very effectively the dangers involved. Many gift shops sell attractively packaged tarot cards and other occult games. Gradually our senses have been dulled. Even if it is just gross commercial exploitation, the result is that a generation has grown up believing that playing with evil powers is just a game.

Some schools are helping to compound this. In one secondary school, first years were taught about voodoo and seances as a part of their Religious Studies course. The textbook they were using gave the Lord's Prayer as an example under the chapter heading 'Communicating with Spirits and God'. One of the tasks set for the class was to make up spells to be recorded on cassette and then played back later to the rest of the class. Not surprisingly, some parents complained to the headmaster. As a result, the textbook was no longer taken home but continued to be used in the classroom.

The inclusion of the occult, in one form or another, in the school curriculum is a difficult issue for Christians to argue against. After all, if these things are a part of our society, then shouldn't young people learn about them? In a secular society where God has been displaced there can ultimately be no right or wrong. As Christians we justifiably feel concerned at the effects learning about such topics may have on the young; but many teachers feel no particular allegiance to God and remain neutral when it comes to spiritual matters. For them the occult is just as much a valid topic of interest as God and Christianity. Some non-Christian teachers would argue that in any case evangelical Christianity could do just as much harm to the individual teenager.

The battle is, of course, much bigger than isolated examples of teenagers playing with ouija boards. Occasionally Christians are woken up to the fact that the devil is fighting fit and wants to bring defeat to God's people – particularly those who are most vulnerable like the young. In one school where there was a large, lively Christian Union numbers suddenly and inexplicably began to dwindle and keen Christians began to lose their enthusiasm, until there was hardly a group left. Later a young man from the school was converted and he told local believers of his involvement with a group that had prayed to evil powers to bring about the downfall of the strong Christian witness in that school. Since then local Christians have renewed their prayers for that school and a Christian group is once again established there.

Christian teenagers are in a battle. Many of them are blissfully unaware of it. Some young believers were taken aback when an older member of the church suggested it was unhelpful for them to be reading their horoscopes from a magazine. They thought at first he must be joking. Whilst Christians sleep, the enemy makes good use of his time and our ignorance. Most of the time he doesn't have to worry about the spectacular. Whilst the pressure of upside-down morals, materialism and secularism are doing their work, Satan doesn't have to resort to the dramatic arts too often.

'Who is Jesus?'

Many schools welcome Christians from outside – particularly ministers or evangelists – to take RE lessons, an assembly or perhaps a sixth-form General Studies period. Such visits take place at the invitation of a teacher or headteacher. The aim is, of course, not to preach or indoctrinate but simply to talk with pupils as representatives of the Christian faith. Opportunities like these are invaluable for encouraging pupils to think through their own beliefs and for helping them to understand more about the Christian faith. Organisations such as Inter School Christian Fellowship and British Youth for Christ have staff, often trained teachers, who are experienced in working in the classroom in this way. The emphasis is on giving a lively, interesting lesson which stimulates genuine discussion and honest thinking about the Christian faith.

'Who is Jesus?' the class was asked.

'He was born in the bulrushes,' said one pupil, trying to be helpful.

'How could he have walked on water when he had holes in his feet?' another thoughtful twelve-year-old wanted to know!

'Jesus never existed – you can't prove it!' said someone else a bit more aggressively.

'Have you ever tried reading about him in the Bible?' the visitor asked.

'Well . . .' giggling and blushing . . . 'No . . .' sinking beneath the desk.

Few teenagers have. Yet many are quick to dismiss Christianity as irrelevant. Jesus Christ was at best just a good man, whilst some, in spite of being shown the writings of secular historians, will still deny that he ever existed.

Many young people who do have some personal interest in Christianity are often not much better acquainted with the Bible and facts of their faith. For a visit to a school Christian group of twelve- and thirteen-year-olds, the speaker had prepared a simple team game based on the story of Bartimaeus. The game was a flop. Hardly anyone in the group had even heard of Bartimaeus. An older group consisting mainly of Christians were asked how many of them read the Bible each day. Out of twenty, only one girl said that she did. At a youth service one Christian boy who was involved in the school Christian Union and attended church regularly, gave the New Testament reading. It was the story of Zacchaeus. He read very well except for the name 'Zacchaeus' which he stumbled over every time. He had clearly never heard the story before.

The appalling ignorance amongst young people about who Jesus is, what Christians believe and what the Bible says is quickly evident on a visit to school. Ask any class, 'Why did Jesus die?' and someone will usually answer, 'To save us from our sins.' Ask what that means and a sea of blank faces will stare back at you, speechless. The phrase has somehow been passed down to them as a kind of folklore which once had a significance, but which has long since been forgotten. Most teenagers today don't know why Jesus Christ came to earth. It's hardly surprising. No longer are children automatically sent to Sunday School; no longer do many schools teach much about the Bible. We can't blame teenagers for their godlessness. They don't know about God or how to find him. The media, school and most adults in society whether inside or outside of school seem to be saying loudly that God, Jesus, the Bible and church are boring and irrelevant and there is no need even to consider the truth about Jesus Christ. So there is now a generation which is growing up with no consciousness of God. Whilst the church continues its usual round of debates, a generation is on course for hell, simply because no one has told them the good news of Jesus.

When young people begin to talk seriously they often express deep-felt anger: anger about the intolerable suffering in the world; anger about all kinds of injustice they see in society. Powerless to hit out against anyone else, God is a name to blame. But more often than not in a classroom discussion people don't even begin to see that Christianity might have some answers. They know from hearsay that churches are uncomfortable and the services boring; school assemblies, RE lessons and the lives of most of their teachers tell them quite clearly that faith in God has little to do with real life. Why then should they take notice of occasional visitors to school who tell them that Christianity is of life and death importance? They must be fanatics. A clutch of third-hand arguments are volunteered by the slightly more interested: 'The Bible is just made-up stories'; 'God couldn't have made the world'; 'The Bible is full of contradictions'. Mostly, though, there is just a great wall of apathy. It often seems as if people were completely deaf; and they wouldn't believe even if hard evidence was produced in front of them. 'Even if it is true, what's it got to do with me?' they ask.

But there is some light in the darkness. In spite of ignorance, in spite of apathy, there are those in every community to whom God is speaking through the Holy Spirit. School is no exception. In one school where there were hardly any Christian pupils, a week of mission was planned. Tim, a sixth former, came to the leaders at the beginning of the week and with a sense of dawning understanding, identified himself with these visiting Christians. About one year before he had begun to feel that there must be more to life than he was experiencing. He went along to chat with his vicar, who gave him a Christian book to read. Somehow Tim knew that he had changed. He had little biblical knowledge, he knew little of current Christian thinking, yet the Holy Spirit was working in his life and teaching him to witness in a pagan world and to recognise others who, like him, had found faith in Christ.

In another school a fourth-year class were listening politely to a visiting Christian. Most of the faces in the class wore the regulation look of boredom until, suddenly, one girl could conceal her interest no longer:

'You really believe in prayer don't you!'

'Yes.'

'Cor! . . . Tell me about prayers he's answered . . .'

The class were amazed to discover that some people

genuinely believed prayer worked. Questions followed thick and fast:

'Do Christians really believe there's no need to be afraid of death?'

'Yes.'

'You can't believe that!'

'Do Christians really believe that God cares about them and is looking after them? What about when things go wrong?'

'Would you still believe God loved you if he let your mum walk under a bus and get killed?'

One of the girls then started explaining rapidly about her mum and dad's marriage break-up and how as a result she was in a foster home and hating it. Did God care about her? The class had been set buzzing not by the objective truths about Christianity, but by their recognition of the genuine belief of those who were talking about it and giving examples of how it worked for them. More importantly, of course, it was the work of the Holy Spirit. Inexplicably a sleepy RE lesson had suddenly exploded into life. Thin concentration had been transformed into rapt attention. There was an alert stillness in the class as if they had a dawning consciousness of truth that was just beyond their grasp.

Often twelve- and thirteen-year-olds are prepared to consider the Christian faith much more rationally and flexibly than older teenagers. One lesson with a friendly RE group was going well. The pupils began to ask their visitors who were leading the lesson, 'How did you become Christians?' The bell for the end of the lesson rang, interrupting the discussion. Books and pens were quickly gathered up. The class was on the move. The teacher pushed the door open and ushered the visitors out into the corridor that was already swarming with hundreds of pupils. Above the crowd of faces and bodies, one small boy was trying to say something to the visitors before they disappeared. He pushed his way through the stream of traffic until he could make himself heard above the noise and then asked simply, 'How can I become a Christian?'

God is at work

Amidst the ignorance and apathy there is emptiness and hunger. God is at work and longs to bring his hope and fullness to those who will recognise his rule in their lives. 'How will they hear without a preacher?' the apostle Paul asks. Whether we are in or out of school, may God give us a glimpse of the suffering of a generation who know nothing of him and prompt us in every way we can to go out to the young and share with them the Bread of Life.

4

Teachers

Teachers come into contact with more unchurched young people than almost any other adults in Britain. As such, they represent tremendous potential for reaching the new generation with the good news of the kingdom. School has a huge impact on most people. Years later we remember tiny details about the people who taught us, our classmates and even things like the distinctive smell of school stew which permeated the whole building on Wednesdays! Christian teachers are a part of that impact. They have the opportunity to bring an awareness of Christianity into school, not just through the narrow responsibilities of their own teaching timetables or involvement in the Christian Union, but through their wider responsibility of contributing to the discussion which shapes the content of the curriculum, the discipline policy and other areas of school life; none are neutral for the Christian and all are part of the profound influence school has in shaping people's future lives. This chapter looks in particular at teacher involvement in the school Christian group, and this may well be an indicator of the level of Christian commitment in other areas of school life.

Missed opportunities

One senior teacher at a school in the south of England reluctantly agreed to allow some mission team members (who also happened to be experienced teachers) into his school to take some sixth-form lessons with the aim of helping them to think seriously about the Christian faith. He eventually mentioned that he, too, was a Christian but liked to keep his faith and professional life separate. Sadly, there are many Christian teachers who have failed to perceive or grasp the opportunities they have to demonstrate their belief in God to their pupils and who lack an expectant, prayerful concern for the young people in their care.

In a large city comprehensive I discovered a Christian Union made up of a handful of dejected fifteen-year-olds. They wanted a lively Christian group that would show their non-Christian friends what faith in Christ really meant. They wanted God to work in their school and had believed he could, but now they had come to the end of their resources. Their meetings had been relegated to a distant room which few people passed. The pressures of keeping going had just become too great. When I asked, 'Are there Christian teachers in school who could help you?' they replied that, yes, there were but they had all said they were too busy to give any time. There were six or seven Christian staff in that school yet they were apparently unable to find a way for even one of them to give some much-needed support to this small, struggling group. This is put into perspective when one hears of some Christian headmasters and deputy heads who, because they believe the visible presence of Christianity in school is so important, regularly give up time to support their school Christian group.

There are many other examples of Christian teachers who have put their faith in a box and do not see its relevance or priority in the school where God has placed them. With this example to follow, it is not surprising that many Christian teenagers find it hard to understand that their faith is something which must permeate the whole of their lives; and it is, therefore, even less surprising that thousands of non-Christian young people are not seeing Christ in their schools.

Available for God

At a time when an increasing number of secondary schools are 11–16 and sixth forms are separate, many school Christian groups desperately need the support and leadership of a Christian staff member. In contrast to the number of teachers who have no sense of God-given vocation, there are many who do have a burning vision of what God wants to do amongst the young and who give of their time, efforts and prayer quite sacrificially in supporting young disciples and in helping others to find faith through their example in life and words. Some of these are commissioned prayerfully to their schools by a local church; others work and pray alone with their churches showing little interest. Most of these teachers would not see themselves as evangelists or 'up-front' speakers; God has simply honoured the time and prayer they have given and as a result many exciting things have happened.

Sue is a good example of what God can do when an 'ordinary' teacher makes herself available to God, not just in terms of her involvement in the CU, but in the way she sees the whole of her professional life as being under God's control. She is head of Religious Education in a small comprehensive school. As far as she knows she is the only committed Christian on the staff. During the last few years she has worked determinedly to restore status to the subject of RE in her school curriculum. Whilst RE is now an accepted examination subject there, it is also abundantly clear to staff and pupils alike that Sue is more concerned with the whole person than mere exam success. There is a sense of life both in Sue's lessons and in her classroom: every centimetre of wall is covered with displays and pupils' work. Discussions are lively and it is obvious that pupils in her classes want to talk because they know the teacher is listening. She works hard at making lessons interesting and enjoyable and is respected and trusted as a teacher by pupils and other staff. As Head of Department she has used her authority to create a syllabus which unashamedly has an emphasis on biblical Christian teaching. Her hard work and obvious concern for her pupils mean that many seek her out to chat or talk over problems. Her classroom is the place where the CU meets – but it is also a safe place where people want to come anyway.

In Christian Union meetings Sue can be more explicit in her teaching. Through her witness in lifestyle and work, she has earned the right to be heard and many young people in that school have listened and decided that they want Sue's God to be their God too. Not only are they converted but they are immediately encouraged to start following Sue's example of prayer and obedience to Jesus' command to 'Go and make disciples . . .'. Young people not yet converted are befriended out of school as well as in school by young members of the CU and are gradually drawn into local church youth fellowships. Whilst Sue is in one sense clearly the leader of this Christian group in school, there is, nevertheless, a strong sense of 'body' and equality. Sue does not make unilateral decisions for the CU, but encourages discussion about how the group should progress and she allows them to make mistakes and, as a result, to learn and grow.

Sue is one of the few who has learnt that faith in Christ invades the whole of an individual's life. She is in the fullest sense a 'Christian teacher'. She is utterly professional, yet her life, character, classroom teaching and extra-curricular activities are making a huge impact on that school community for Christ.

Making disciples

Many of the teachers who have the clearest sense of God's call to serve him in a particular school and who are doing so very effectively are often the most self-effacing of people. They do not seek an authoritarian style of leadership of the young Christians in their school. Instead their rock hard certainty of a God who cares deeply for all individuals sets free young disciples in school to take responsibility and the initiative in demonstrating the gospel in a variety of ways.

In the last few years another teacher, Mark, has done a tremendous work amongst boys from the city where he works. His deep concern led him to begin annual camps for teenage boys from local schools. The aim of these camps was to introduce unchurched teenagers to Jesus Christ. Hundreds of boys passed through those camps and many have become Christians as a result. Mark's vision did not stop at the point of conversion. Like Sue, he was concerned to see young Christians growing. Boys converted one year would be given some responsibility in leading the following year. Partly as a result of his enthusiastic example, some school Christian Unions in the city began going out at lunchtime to other schools to present the gospel at a meeting hosted by the 'home' CU. Gradually links were formed amongst Christians in schools throughout the area and a united sense of concern for non-Christians at school developed amongst the teenagers. Mark's leadership had far-reaching consequences. He wasn't a one-man show. Rather he enabled many young believers to take responsibility and be the witnesses both individually and corporately that God wanted them to be.

The results of Mark's openness to God have been quite dramatic. Just as important are the less spectacular groups of believers who are enabled, through the patient and faithful service of one teacher, to sustain a quiet witness in a school that would otherwise have no Christian influence. For example, Katherine was newly qualified and had a deep sense of God's call to be a teacher. She couldn't understand why she had had no success in finding a first post ready for the Autumn term. She began to wonder if she had got her guidance confused. Meanwhile, in Cornwall a small group of girls were praying for a Christian teacher to join the staff of their school. They had a strong commitment to Jesus Christ but felt desperate for some adult support. So they had started praying that God would send them a Christian teacher. Katherine had in fact done her teaching practice in that same school the previous Spring term, but the pupils didn't know that she was still looking for a job. Unexpectedly, a teacher left, creating a vacancy for the next Spring term. Amazingly the headmaster remembered Katherine and contacted her to find out if she had a job and if not whether she would like one! A lovely example of God matching his people's prayers: Katherine had the right job and the Christian pupils in that school had the support they needed so much. Her presence meant that a quiet but consistent Christian witness was continued there.

Christian teachers are often the key to an effective school Christian group. They are able to give the necessary confidence and vision to young Christians. Their presence gives the group a greater sense of recognition and acceptance in the school as a whole. They can also provide continuity when a group of particularly lively pupil leaders leave school. The happiest and most enthusiastic of groups seem to result when teachers don't see themselves as 'boss' but as 'co-worker', a fellow member of

Christ's body and a servant of both the Christian and the non-Christian in school. With this attitude young people are helped to take responsibility for prayer and witness and to understand that God wants to reach out through them in love to all those who don't yet know him.

Fellow-Christians

Some Christian teachers fear the openness that should exist between Christians in school. After all it demolishes the barriers between teacher and pupil, between the young and adults. They fear that it will mean a loss of professionalism or appear to show favouritism to Christians. Both of these pitfalls have been avoided by many teachers. The qualities of humility and love in a teacher who recognises Christian pupils as fellow members of Christ's body and non-Christian pupils as fellow sinners are often revealed more in unspoken attitudes and actions than in words. Most young people have more good sense than we often credit them with; for the most part, they are able to cope with the mixture of an adult who is both brother in Christ and teacher. There are many ways in which teachers can be both open-hearted with fellow Christians and at the same time utterly professional and not break confidences.

Recently, at a CU meeting in Suffolk, a Christian teacher who was a head of year in that school, arrived late. The group was about to start praying for one another's needs. The teacher apologised for being late and then, out of an obvious sense of need for God's help and belief that God would hear the prayers of this young group, he explained simply that he had had a very difficult morning with hard decisions to make. He had told no secrets, but through his openness, discretion and humility in admitting his need, he had demonstrated the oneness of the Body of Christ where there is no place for elitism. He had also set an example for these young people in their turn to follow.

Feel like giving up!

Some teachers may feel that some of the examples of Christian groups described here are exceptions and that really there is no hope for the small group of Christians in their school. The group will never be able to or want to take responsibility for its own activities. They may be such a stodgy lot, that it's a good thing that no one else comes, because they would probably be put off Christianity for life! Equally you haven't the energy or time to do much more than take the once-a-week half-hour meeting.

There are, of course, many school Christian Unions where there seem to be few pupils with any spark and there seems to be little hope that the group will change. There are several dangers in this situation. The teacher may come to see the CU simply as a duty; an attitude which tends to creep up unnoticed and which leads to dullness and stultification. It becomes just another club rather than something which is about living relationships. The staff member falls back on the traditional teacher/pupil roles and the young people, as a result, are not helped to see the change which being a part of God's family brings. Also, the teacher begins to organise everything because it seems easier that way; and so the young people are not encouraged to see that God expects something of them too.

In the case of Sue and her school Christian group, none of the young people there were older than fifteen and none of the group were obvious leaders. Sue helped them develop a sense of being Christ's body and a sense of responsibility by patiently and painstakingly drawing them into decision-making. She would talk with enthusiasm about ideas for the group and their witness in school and then set the choices before them, encouraging discussion about the options and helping them to make decisions. In a recent mission, the young Christians working with Sue alongside them, organised the meeting room for each lunchtime, produced endless cups of coffee and washed up afterwards, drew countless posters and displayed them all over school, gave helpful contributions in classroom discussions, manned a bookstall at breaktimes and brought their non-Christian friends to the meetings. It was very much their mission. They quite unashamedly identified themselves with

Christianity in front of the rest of the school. But it was Sue, the teacher, supported by the prayers of several local churches, who was the key to releasing them in service.

With quiet, shy groups who seem reluctant to contribute anything, it is easy to give up. God, of course, does not give up and the Bible makes it quite clear that he wants all his people to be used in the work of his kingdom; that means young Christians as well as adults. Prayer does change situations and many Christian teachers who have felt perhaps for several years that the CU in their school could never be dynamic, have been surprised when the Holy Spirit has suddenly touched the lives of some of the young people, bringing his life into an apparently hopeless situation, as a result of people's prayer. Even if young people seem as if they will never take the lead themselves, at least in our minds we need prayerfully to hold firm to the aim of helping them to take responsibility. Ephesians 3:20 gives some encouragement when it describes God like this: 'To him who . . . is able to do so much more than we can ever ask for, or even think of . . .' (GNB). How much are the local Christians in your area asking God for their school? Well, he can do much more! One of the dangers of giving up hope is that we don't recognise signs of growth when they come.

On a visit to one Christian Union, I was met by a teacher who told me about the Christian staff's irritation with the programme planned by the pupil committee: 'We've told them it won't work,' she said, 'but they won't change it. See if you can persuade them.' Later, talking with the pupil committee, they said with frustration, 'The trouble is we plan a meeting carefully and have just got going, when the teachers come in and take over.' Quite a communication problem! The teachers really wanted to be in charge just as they were in the classroom. They hadn't recognised that it was healthy that the pupils were taking the lead and had been creative in their thinking about serving God. Both teachers and pupils saw it as an 'us and them' situation not seeing that those rules don't apply in the kingdom of God. Even if the committee did make mistakes at least they had a sense of commitment and involvement which would have been lost if they had simply allowed the teachers to take over.

Leadership is costly

To return to Sue for a moment, it is worth remembering that her style of leadership was extremely time-consuming both in and out of school. Also, it was Sue's own enthusiasm for the gospel, her evident belief that knowing Jesus Christ is of supreme importance and her belief that each individual human being is of great worth that were the prime inspiration to the young Christians in that school to be enthusiastic themselves about the good news of Jesus Christ. Sue's life was also marked with quiet joy and a sense of humour, in spite of a difficult personal life, making it clear that she was someone very much at peace with her God. It is a costly business being available for God to use in school, but if as adults we genuinely want to see God at work there, then first we must allow God to work in our own lives and bring his renewal to us.

Why so much emphasis on teacher involvement in the CU in any case? Can't an individual teacher's witness be seen simply in their work? Some teachers like the one in the example at the beginning of this chapter don't seem to believe that their faith has much to do with their school life. Brian Hill writes in his excellent book, *Faith at the Blackboard* (page 67):

> Christian teachers are often insufficiently alert to the opportunity of being involved in voluntary Christian fellowships on school premises with their students and others whom they don't themselves teach in class. After all, the catchment of the public (state) school is *all* young people of educable age in the adjacent community ... When the Christian teacher is faced with the issue of priorities in the involvement of his own time and talents, he should ask himself this question: Who else has as good or better access than I do to the unchurched youth population gathered on public (state) school premises?

By meeting with the CU the teacher identifies himself publicly in front of colleagues and pupils with the cause of Christ. Some teachers seem sadly reluctant to do this. Yet, the presence of a teacher will provide encouragement for young Christians in school who are trying to live for Christ in a difficult environment. The teacher's participation in the group will mean that some young believers who haven't previously seen the need to demonstrate their faith in school are drawn out to do so by meeting with the CU. The teacher's presence may also mean that some unchurched young people will see it as something with status and worth attending.

Members of one family

Finally, all Christians are members of the *one* family of God. Paul had to remind Philemon (the master) and Onesimus (the slave) of this fact. Throughout the centuries Christians have had an inborn impulse to come together because of that oneness, because they recognised the necessity of this if they were to survive and because they had a common concern and message for those around them who were going to hell. In our well-cushioned, cosy Christian world many believing Christian teachers seem to have lost their natural family love for one another. Often we seem content to waste time in sophistication, cynical attitudes to fellow Christians and arguments over trivial differences with other members of God's family, rather than getting on with the task in hand. The Bible makes it clear that Christians are least effective when alone: 'For where two or three come together in my name, there am I with them' (Matthew 18:20), says Jesus to us. That means in school too. Of course, Christian teachers, pupils, the caretaker, the caterer and the lab assistants are all called to live for Christ as individuals in school, but there is surely something wrong if they don't want, if possible, to find one another out and in some way come together to pray and work together in what is a distinctly pagan environment. Difficulties and barriers there may be but with the Holy Spirit's help these can be overcome.

Often reasons given by teachers for total non-involvement in the school CU are just excuses for not taking seriously the fact that it is God who has placed them in that school for his good purposes. It is easy also to see involvement in the CU only in terms of giving, whereas the pressures which are on the pupils

61

are similar to those which face the teachers and they need to receive the encouragement of fellow Christians just as much as their younger brothers and sisters. One teacher recounted the following incident of a young Christian pupil encouraging her. The teacher had had a particularly difficult day and as a result she was unnecessarily sharp with one of her classes. At the end of the lesson a young Christian girl came up to her and asked with genuine concern, much to the teacher's chagrin and some amusement, whether she had had a 'quiet time' that morning! Teachers need to set the appropriate example; if they don't, how will young Christians ever take up the challenge of costly discipleship? Some teachers may also be surprised to find that the simple faith and dynamism of some Christian teenagers has much to teach them.

One senior staff member of a school replied to a letter from an Inter School Christian Fellowship worker encouraging him to start a CU, by saying something like this: 'There are several Christian teachers in this school. We did try to start a Christian group a few years ago, but no one was interested, so there is no point in trying again. In any case, most of us are involved in youth groups in the town, so we don't really see the need for anything in school.' This teacher could only see a CU as another club, like the drama or chess club. This one person, because of his defeatism, his lack of understanding of himself as a member of God's family and of the opportunities to share his faith in school, was a block to the potential growth of all young Christians in that school and the witness which, if a Christian group had been formed, could have resulted to the many, many unchurched young people in that place.

Getting organised

Attending every CU meeting or organising the programme is by no means the only way in which Christian teachers can identify with and express support for other Christians in school. Some busy Christian headmasters or deputy heads do not have time to attend CU meetings regularly, but nevertheless very successfully give their support to the young Christians by giving practical help, by making a point of talking with the CU leaders from time to time or by going into a CU lunch for a few moments occasionally. Some school Christian groups function very effectively without much staff organisation, although they do have a considerable sense of staff support. Pupils may be inhibited if several staff members regularly turn up to meetings, so if there are a number of Christian staff it is probably wise to try and arrange that they don't all come to the same meetings.

In some schools where there are a large number of Christian teachers and a CU which clearly needs staff leadership, the teachers have agreed that perhaps two of them will take responsibility for the group and the others will pray. This arrangement may have a time limit, perhaps of one or two years, when others will take a turn. This doesn't preclude the other teachers from attending CU meetings and certainly oneness with and concern for Christian pupils in school will be expressed as all of them pray about the witness of the family of God in that place. Support can be shown in numerous ways through, for example, taking opportunities to chat informally with young Christians. All Christian staff can make it known that they are available to give help or advice, all can make an effort to publicise CU events and all can use their influence for the good of the CU in the staffroom.

If there are several Christian staff members in a school there should be no question of everyone being too busy to show an interest and also no need for a keen, but overworked probationary teacher to have to take on the extra burden of planning a CU programme. If, on the other hand, there is only one Christian teacher in that school then the responsibility clearly rests with that person to get involved, and to take up the offensive for the cause of God's kingdom.

Sometimes there are no voluntary Christian activities in a school because there are few committed Christian pupils. As a response to this many Christian teachers and senior pupils have started lunchtime clubs for first and second years with the aim of introducing them to the Christian message through activities and teaching. Often a smaller fellowship group may result for those who have a deeper interest. Hopefully, as some of the young people are converted, they will form the nucleus of a Christian Union as they go up through the school and over a number of years a Christian witness will be established. This kind of junior Christian activity for first and second years provides one of the invaluable opportunities Christian teachers have for contact with young people who would never normally go near a church, but who are happy to come to an enjoyable informal meeting with their friends in school.

Faith at work

''Ere Miss, you're always sayin' how bein' a Christian gives you peace an' that, so 'ow come on a Monday morning when you walk in to take our class you're so nervous, you've got your fists clenched?' Paul, cheeky and friendly out of class, was always ready to talk; but in class he could be one of the least co-operative and most obstreperous of a difficult class of fourth-years, who in general viewed school as a waste of time and consequently tried to make it as entertaining as possible for themselves at the teacher's expense. As a young probationary teacher I dreaded my regular meeting with this mischievous group first thing every Monday morning and then two more times during the week. A discussion had arisen about Christianity and not wanting to be open to the charge of indoctrination I had suggested that anyone who wanted to could stay on at the end of school to continue the discussion informally. Paul had been one of those who stayed on to explain why he didn't believe in God and to point out with devastating, youthful frankness that he didn't think my life, in certain respects, matched up to what I said about the Christian faith.

As soon as a Christian teacher identifies himself, he makes himself vulnerable. Perhaps that is one reason why many Christian teachers aren't prepared to let their pupils and colleagues know about their faith. It is the whole of one's life that counts. Young people might not know the facts about Christianity, but they know what they expect from a Christian teacher; and teachers, being human, make mistakes. In spite of that they do have tremendous power because young people watch their lives carefully. Justice, fairness, kindness, respect for the individual and getting homework marked on time are all qualities highly valued by teenagers in their teachers and are a most important part of the Christian teacher's demonstration of what their faith is all about.

As well as tremendous opportunities to share Christ, teachers also have pressures: not only from the young people they teach, but also from the colleagues they work with. The young Christian teacher comes to his work with high ideals, but often finds himself amongst those who have lost them altogether or who have very different values. There are those who are aggressively ambitious, the cynical who have seen it all before and the trendy ones who regularly spend lunchtime down at the local. In the staffroom, discussion about the pupils doesn't always seem to be too caring. This is not to say, of course, that there aren't many non-Christian teachers who are highly motivated and deeply concerned for the young people in their care. But it does mean that the Christian's ideals can quickly crash about his ears. Nevertheless his influence in staff meetings can be of utmost importance as he puts a Christian viewpoint forward in discussions about curriculum, syllabus and pastoral care. Sometimes this means standing alone.

Many Christian teachers meet together in school to pray for one another, for the young Christians in school and for the school in general and this both gives support and increases their sense of God's involvement in that place and their awareness of opportunities of bringing Christ into school.

In the front line

At the beginning of this chapter I pointed out that teachers have more access to unchurched young people than almost any other class of adults. Teachers are a huge resource for the witness of the church to the large section of the local community who are at school. It seems, therefore, totally illogical that whilst Christians in this country commission in a very definite way 'missionaries' to teach in schools overseas – schools which very often will have a strong Christian foundation and a praying staff – they ignore teachers in this country who work week by week in largely pagan establishments where they are constantly under fire for their

Christian beliefs and witness. Teachers are in the front line of missionary work amongst the young and many of them aren't even aware of it. They are in desperate need of support and encouragement from the church for the clear missionary task that God has given them. They in their turn can then give the lead to teenage Christians and with them work at making Christ and his kingdom known in our schools.

5

Classroom Christians

A Christian teenager has up to five or six years to demonstrate the worth of his faith to his fellow pupils. After that time many non-Christians will have had ample opportunity to decide whether the words of a Christian match his life. Many of the young people who were converted whilst at school will say it was because of the lives of their Christian friends – there was something different about them; they genuinely cared about other people.

Christian teenagers wanting to share their faith in school, shouldn't be trapped into thinking that it is only their words that matter. You don't have to be a gifted speaker or know all the answers to difficult questions to be an effective witness for Jesus Christ. Living in obedience to Christ and consequently making decisions which are different from other people's because you are a believer, will in the end provoke more comment, genuine questions and interest than verbal argument ever will. We live in a self-centred society and unselfish acts of kindness and concern for others stand out. Over a period of time some people will want to know the reasons behind the actions.

A day in a life

Direct, easily recognisable attacks on our faith are, in some ways, the easiest to withstand. But there are many more subtle ways in which our witness can be unobtrusively undermined and destroyed. For the young person at school the pressure is on to follow the crowd; but Christ calls the Christian to follow him. Each day presents a string of choices which test the faith and witness of the disciple.

The first test of the day may be arriving at school on time. Even if you manage to get up early enough, you still might be late because you give in to the temptation to hang around chatting with friends in the cloakroom before going to registration. Fellow pupils will be only too happy to remind the Christian that arriving late doesn't fit in with his 'Christian' standards and the teacher will notice too. A headmaster in a Suffolk school introduced a visitor who had come to speak at assembly to the head boy. After he had gone the head said to the visitor, 'He's a good lad, but never on time'. The head boy was a Christian and in a small way his regular lateness diminished his testimony to the headmaster.

Perhaps later in the morning the young believer is part of a class that is in a disruptive mood. It's all too easy to join in with everyone else making life difficult for the teacher, or at least to sit back and not make much effort to work. Few Christian teenagers are aware of the contribution they can make towards establishing a good atmosphere if they continue to work quietly and cheerfully in an unsettled class. Even school work is not just for the teacher, not just for parents, not even for the pupil himself, but it is for God and that should be a stimulus to aim for the highest standards possible at all times. Even one Christian's behaviour in a classful of non-Christians does have an influence on the way others work. Kindness, courtesy and good work are a witness to the teacher too who is just as much in need of Christ as fellow pupils.

At breaktime all sorts of challenges to the believer arise which may all too easily pass unnoticed. Do you immediately hive off with your cronies and yet again leave the lonely, the shy and the misfits to wander awkwardly around school or hide in an empty classroom? Do you seek out Christian friends and so avoid any contact with non-Christians? On the other hand do you go along with the in-crowd and end up by appearing to agree with conversation which in your heart of hearts makes you ashamed?

Lunchtime comes around. There's a CU meeting; do you go to it and risk the PE teacher's disapproval for missing another hockey practice, or do you play hockey and end up feeling guilty for letting down fellow Christians? On the other hand, perhaps you see hockey as a priority, something which you feel God wants you to be involved in. But you are still a member of God's family in school, so how are you going to keep up your links with other Christians? Then, if you are at sixth form college, there is probably a small group of students who tell you that 'everyone' is going to the pub. It is easy to persuade yourself that as that is where the non-Christians are, you should be there too, although if you are honest that is not the real reason you want to go.

In an afternoon lesson a lively discussion on abortion or nuclear disarmament develops. Do you sit back quietly or try to join in with a specifically Christian viewpoint? In lessons and informal conversations in school, the Christian has the opportunity to show that God is concerned with every area of thought and life and is not just reserved for a Sunday-only box. That means that Christian teenagers have got to do some hard thinking about all sorts of topical issues: CND, feminism, fashion and music, for instance. What guidance does the Bible give on these issues? Facing up to the challenge of the rule of God's word in your life may be costly. Far more opportunities arise naturally to discuss important issues during our teens than perhaps at any other time of life.

Each day at school decisions about these and many other choices give opportunity for the believer's faith in Christ to be seen and heard or to be quietly undermined and forgotten. How can he cope? The answer is the age-old one of a close relationship with Jesus Christ founded in regular personal Bible reading and prayer. All too many Christians have been taught to expect someone else to do the job for them: to provide the teaching, to provide the evangelism for their friends. As a result, sadly many teenagers aren't honestly bothered about making Jesus known to their contemporaries – it is someone else's job. But God calls Christian teenagers, as well as adults, to take responsibility for their own relationship with him and to answer his call to go and make disciples.

Teachers need Christ too

It is easy to forget that teachers may be just as provoked or interested by the witness of Christian pupils as their classmates. Teachers are, for example, quick to notice who doesn't give in homework on time. Many a Christian teacher has been disappointed when a non-Christian colleague has concluded his grumbling about this with, '. . . and isn't he one of your Christian Union lot?'

In one school a backslidden Christian staff member admitted to the teacher responsible for the CU that the clearly changed lives of two hitherto difficult girls who had been befriended by Christians had convicted him and made him reconsider the claims of Christ on his life.

In another school there was a non-Christian teacher of Religious Education who disliked intensely the views of some keen young Christians in his classes. He had studied theology at Cambridge and felt that his pupils couldn't teach him anything. Wisely, they didn't try to argue with him, but they did pray. Eventually, personal problems brought him to a crisis point. He knew that his Christian pupils had something which he lacked. Bravely, he decided to go to their church, where he found Christ. He joined with other Christians at school in the CU and is now working as a missionary overseas. Teachers need Christ too.

Come together

Actions provoke questions, but words are needed as well, if people are to receive answers and understand the gospel message. Scattered individual Christians in a school community of perhaps 1,500 cannot hope to be heard by many or make much of an impact. For the lone Christian teenager, no matter how good his intentions, it is hard not to be swept along by the crowd or just to protect himself by fading quietly into the background or hiding behind work.

Believers have always sought each other out and spontaneously come together, because of that sense of being one family and of having unity of purpose in an alien world. It is the same for many young Christians in school today. They naturally want to come together for mutual support and in order to share their faith in the midst of a community that is often openly antagonistic to Christianity. As a result, throughout Britain hundreds of small and large groups of teenage believers regularly meet together in schools.

A group of dedicated teenagers coming together for fellowship and to pray is at the heart of effective, powerful witness to the school community. This whole generation captive on our doorsteps, this huge secular community, is unlikely to be reached by one struggling, solitary Christian, but can be touched by the united voice of a group of thirty or forty young people who work and pray together.

One Christian boy in Wales wanted very much to share Christ with the people in his school. But other Christian teenagers showed little interest. By himself he set up a 'Christian Union' and planned a programme. He regularly put up posters around school to advertise the CU and invited outside speakers to take meetings to which a small number of people would come. Whilst on the one hand these efforts deserve respect and praise, on the other, this is a sad example. The 'Christian Union' was known as the work of this one lad and as such it was something of a curiosity, not to be taken too seriously. By contrast, a united, lively, well-organised large group of Christian teenagers will be noticed and will bring with it an unmistakeable Christian presence into school.

God never intended his people to live and work alone. In the New Testament the word 'you' is rarely in the singular; instead it refers to the community of God's people. Being a part of God's family is a privilege and a blessing – it means I don't need to struggle and fail (or succeed) alone. It is also a discipline: I may not like my brothers and sisters, but I have a responsibility to love them, to learn from them, give to them and be a worker with them. Jesus prayed in the Garden of Gethsemane for those who would believe on him in the future: '. . . that all of them may be one . . . to let the world know that you sent me . . .' (John 17:20–23). Earlier Jesus had told his disciples: 'All men will know that you are my disciples if you love one another' (John 13:35). Coming together with other Christians in school is not just an optional extra for the health and happiness of the individual. It is, as these verses show, a key factor in making Jesus known.

As Christians meet together they have the opportunity to demonstrate a pattern of values and relationships which is in

71

sharp contrast to those of the larger community. Individually they cannot do this so easily, but the different attitudes, values and friendship of a group of people will be seen and provoke comment. Why should a bright, popular sixth former be friends with an insignificant second-year? Why should a good-looking fifth-year boy appear to be just good friends with an attractive fourth-year girl and not 'going out' with her? Why should John, who is really quite a laugh, have so much time and respect for that rather quiet, boring teacher? Age, intelligence, common interests, personality, status – all of these are nothing to do with the fundamental oneness of Christians. This acceptance of one another takes non-Christians by surprise and is a major puzzle. They see something they want in their own lives.

Members of one Christian Union gave up a whole Saturday to paint a particularly ugly wall in their school. It was a wall which everyone passed regularly and it looked a mess. So the CU decided that painting it would cheer school life up. They had a great day together and everyone knew that it was the Christians who had done it.

Visible signs of love and acceptance between people and tangible acts of service for others build the platform from which the CU can speak to the school about their faith and reasons for belief with credibility. Fellowship, service and witness go together.

Objectives for the Christian Union

The characteristics of a Christian group as outlined above are, of course, ideals, but they are present to some extent in all fellowships of God's people because the Holy Spirit is at work in the lives of all believers. From time to time a Christian group is particularly blessed and particularly obedient and for a year or two it emerges as a noticeable force in school with many being converted.

One group in Devon became the talk of the school, staff and pupils, simply because of the life they demonstrated. It consisted of thirteen- to eighteen-year-olds with a fair balance of boys and girls. The friendship and openness between them showed

72

clearly as did their joy, dynamic sense of purpose and sparkling sense of fun. They met regularly to pray, praise, learn and witness together. A newly converted teacher was helped in his early steps as a Christian through the group's careful nurture and encouragement. Other teachers, impressed by the strength of commitment and clarity of thought of some of the older members, invited them to take part in some RE lessons to talk to other pupils about their reasons for belief. The group organised its own week of mission in the school, as a result of which about a dozen pupils professed faith in Christ.

People didn't necessarily agree with all that they said, but they couldn't help liking them. They were the sort of people you wanted to be with. Everything about them spoke life. Non-Christians wanted to discover why this group of people were so attractively different.

Sadly, this is not a typical description of many school CUs. One problem is that the original reasons for meeting as a Christian group get forgotten. The CU continues to meet out of habit or duty, but has lost all sense of life and purpose. As a result the group meetings become boring and unattractive. Or, if aims aren't clearly defined, the group's programme can become unbalanced so that neither the needs of Christians or non-Christians are met.

A Retreat?

Ask any group why they meet together in school and most will reply that it is because they want to support each other. The difficulties of being a Christian at school mean that meeting with other Christians in the middle of a busy day can give much needed encouragement. Even those who are not very good at speaking about their faith show just by going to the CU, which in some schools is a brave thing to do, that they believe Christianity is important. This silent statement to classmates may well be more effective than many words from adults.

For some, however, the CU is not just about fellowship, it has become, in addition, an exclusive retreat from an unkind world. The group described in an earlier chapter who on one occasion had stones thrown at them as they went to a CU meeting, felt a real dread of the community in which they found themselves.

73

They loved the Lord and there was a strong bond of friendship between them, but they had come to see those outside their group as 'the enemy'. Particularly for teenagers who are growing up in a protective Christian family, the non-Christian community of school can seem frightening. If they are growing up with a strong allegiance to Christian values, the behaviour of their contemporaries may seem impossible to understand as well as frightening. This fear and lack of understanding can obliterate any sense of compassion or love for those without Christ.

The group which makes fellowship an excuse for retreat, communicates to outsiders that Christianity is for a small number of people who have rather peculiar ideas and who dislike those who are not just like them. If the group are reading the Bible and praying together then these spiritual resources have no outlet, unless the group changes its attitudes and moves out into school. The retreat mentality stultifies effective witness and the spiritual growth of individual Christians. The group that only looks inward will eventually die. The purpose of true fellowship in a school Christian group is to provide the strength, love and motivation necessary for effective witness, as the group move out into school and act as salt – in class, in sports, in drama and wherever members find themselves.

Some groups tell you that they don't feel ready yet for 'witness'; meanwhile they are concentrating on 'fellowship'. There is a basic misunderstanding here of what witness is about. It is seen as a limited activity that you decide to do for a certain length of time. Jesus called his disciples to *be* witnesses – not to do witness. All believers are witnesses, good or bad, whether they like it or not. Those groups who plan to wait until they feel 'strong' enough to talk about the gospel, probably never will. Morris Stuart makes the point that for the disciples of Jesus mission was the context for learning: 'His (Jesus') context was mission, and nurture of his disciples was a function within that wider context'. When teenagers take up the responsibility of making Jesus known and see themselves as workers together with God, the result is growth and a sense of purpose and joy in the lives of individuals. How then does the CU set about the task of taking the message of Jesus Christ to those outside the church?

74

The existence of the CU in itself is a reminder to the whole school that people of the teenage generation believe the Christian faith to be important. The witness of the Christians is more than just what happens in a CU meeting. The CU, however, is the focal point for Christians in school; it is the means through which they come together and are seen as an identifiable body in school. Going out as a recognised member of that body, the young believer consciously seeks to live for Christ, apart from, but supported by, his fellow Christians, taking the life of Christ into the activities of the school day. Teenagers need to develop a consciousness of and a compassion for the needs of the hundreds of young people around them who don't know God. Meeting as the Christian Union can do this and help them to understand that God has a purpose in placing them in a particular school. It can also give them the confidence to believe that God doesn't just use adults but wants to use them as well to bring their friends to Christ. Teenagers taken up with this understanding can become a daunting force.

The balanced CU programme will include some meetings which are intended to explain the gospel to non-Christians; for example, a visiting speaker or CU members who talk about their reasons for faith. But not all of these meetings need to be specifically 'evangelistic'. Some may, for example, take the form of a discussion on a topical issue at which there is the opportunity to put forward a Christian viewpoint. Bridges of understanding need to be built slowly. Sometimes non-Christians need to be welcomed to an event put on by the Christians which is simply for enjoyment; for example, organising pancake races on Shrove Tuesday! Many meetings will be intended for the Christians, but should be seen as the starting line and pit-stop for their witness. There need to be regular times when Christians can talk about the difficulties or encouragements they are finding in living as Christians in school; times when they can pray for one another and for each other's non-Christian friends; times when they study the Bible together and apply the challenge of what they are learning directly to their lives in school.

Just as keen young Christians, guided and supported, can be a powerful force in making Christ known in school, so over-enthusiastic young Christians with no spiritually mature leadership can be a powerful force to bring Christianity into disrepute both with pupils and staff. Some CUs have even been closed down by worried headmasters because teenagers have been irresponsible in their 'witnessing'.

For example, Christians have arrived late at lessons because they were having an important conversation. In one school minor hysteria broke out because of the way in which Christians told some sensitive teenage girls they were going to hell. A fifth year boy twisted the title of an essay in his English mock O-level exam so that he could preach a mini-sermon; the essay was bad by any standard. Fortunately, the teacher who marked it was a Christian. Whilst the young Christians in these situations were revelling in what they mistakenly believed to be the 'cost' of discipleship they were oblivious to the poor witness given by their lack of punctuality and low standards of work. Meanwhile the staff were becoming dismissive of the CU and concerned at the disruptiveness of its activities. Being a Christian doesn't exempt us from using a little common sense. As well as being insensitive, these Christians were simply not fulfilling their responsibilities as pupils and consequently bringing their witness into disrepute. They were not suffering for their faith. As Jesus said, we are to: 'Give to Caesar what is Caesar's and to God what is God's' (Mark 12:17). Teenage Christians do sometimes need help in getting the balance right. However, the danger of being over-zealous isn't a major problem for most groups.

Variety in the programme is all-important if the life and witness of the CU is to be kept healthy and attractive. The various elements of fellowship, outreach, learning together, prayer and service all need to be present. With each of these there is, of course, the danger of over-emphasis on any one aspect. Too much stress on fellowship can lead to an inward-looking group; too much emphasis on outreach can lead to a loss of concentration on school work. However, service is an aspect of the CU's activities which seems to have faded from the consciousness of many school groups and it is perhaps time to redress the balance.

Service
Some Christian teachers leading CUs may be afraid of giving the

impression that the Christian Union is simply a group of 'do-gooders'. They may feel that their energies should be wholly directed to feeding the young Christians and helping them to make Christ known in direct ways. Yet 'service' is a part of all that. It shows that believers not only care about the quality of all life, but that they are prepared to give time and effort to do something about it; they are not just interested in notching up converts. Those who are not Christians need to understand that Christians will serve them, not as a carrot to tempt them to become Christians, but because it is the nature of Christ to give unreservedly without expecting anything in return.

In our individualistic society where so many feel isolated, anything which Christians can do to build up a sense of community in school and people's sense of belonging to it, is a valuable act of service. For example, the group who painted the wall were showing that school was a place they felt they belonged to, a place in which they wanted to take pride. What they did was an example of care for the community which others might be motivated to follow. The pancake races organised by another school involved teachers and pupils from all levels; crowds of people gathered round the races held at lunchtime and enjoyed eating pancakes that CU members were cooking and selling. The event was simply social, put on for fun, but it helped to build up the sense of community life in that school. Both these examples also communicated in quiet ways that Christians enjoy life and want other people to do so too. They were 'bridge-builders', so that when the next posters went up to advertise a CU meeting, non-Christians wouldn't feel quite so afraid of going.

Service should, of course, also include thinking about and giving to areas outside the immediate province of school. Sharing with other believers or needy people in other parts of the world can enrich and widen the teenagers' vision of their own community and their part in it.

Who Leads?

Joanne, at twelve, had managed to gather together a group of sympathetic friends and persuaded a not-very-enthusiastic RE teacher to allow them to form a Christian group in school. The teacher had also been persuaded to allow a speaker into school to take their first meeting. The teacher wasn't quite sure what to make of it all; meanwhile, Joanne's face shone with excitement throughout that meeting.

Judy, a reserved, not very bright fourteen-year-old knew of no other committed Christians in the senior part of her school. Feeling that there should be some kind of Christian group established, she organised and led regular meetings for first- and second-years.

Sandra, a bubbly, intelligent upper sixth-form student, conscientiously trained and prepared younger, less confident pupils to take over the leadership of the CU from her for several months before she left.

When the word 'leadership' is mentioned we tend to think of adults. In school it is easy to think that only teachers can lead. Yet experience shows that God uses people – the young, the old, the intelligent and not-so-intelligent – who want to serve him, know him, make him known and be obedient. When God said, 'Who will go for us?' (Isaiah 6:8), he didn't add a long list of qualifications and conditions. Isaiah simply overheard the question and responded in the affirmative. The most effective CU leaders are likely to be enthusiastic teenagers who will communicate that enthusiasm for God to fellow Christians and non-Christians alike. They are the ones who know best the culture of their peers. Christian teachers can offer support and guidance from behind.

A problem arises when keen CU leaders leave school: the Christian witness might go too, if there are no obvious leaders to continue the group. This is one reason why a partnership in leadership between staff and pupils is so important. The Christian teacher may from time to time need to become more prominent in his leadership of the group, depending on the abilities and confidence of the pupils who make up the CU, but constantly working to involve pupils in taking decisions and responsibility for themselves. If possible, pupils from all years need to be involved in the leadership so that the group isn't seen just as one particular teacher's interest, but as something which springs from the lives and initiative of the pupils themselves.

In some schools there is an all-pupil committee of perhaps fifth and sixth formers who plan the programme and carry out practical arrangements. Here the staff stay in the background making it clear that help and advice are always available, but supporting mainly through prayer and verbal encouragement. In other schools one Christian teacher is appointed each year to the committee holding equal status with the pupil members. Some CU committees include at least one representative from each year. This has the advantage of constantly training a leadership so that the Christian witness in a school can be maintained over the years.

Unfortunately, a teacher occasionally sees himself as the only possible leader, irrespective of the qualities of the younger members of the group. Spontaneity, enthusiasm and initiative are crushed and eventually real life may die. Christians and non-Christians alike don't want to be a part of a group like this; meanwhile the teacher becomes embittered at the lack of support the group is given.

Training for the Future

Isn't it dangerous and unwise to encourage young people to lead? Don't they make huge mistakes? In the vast majority of cases the answer is no, and if they do make mistakes, isn't it better for them to learn early for themselves rather than later? Responsibility develops a greater sense of responsibility. A minister who has taken a break from church work to undertake some study, confessed how, now that he is no longer under the watchful eye of his congregation, he finds it much harder to choose to do the right thing. Being a Christian leader of any sort acts as a spur to live a holier, more Christ-centred life. Service brings fruit and maturity. When young people organise a Bible study or a prayer meeting for themselves, they are more likely to feel involved in it, to understand the reasons behind it and learn from it, than if it was laid on for them by adult leaders.

The school CU can provide an invaluable training ground in leading and organising. The commitment that good CU leadership demands captures and develops the potential of young Christians and will make them better prepared for future service in God's kingdom.

Objections

Why Have a Christian Union?

Some ministers, parents and young people argue that there is
no need for a Christian group to be meeting in school anyway,
if the church is doing its job properly. Some young people will
say, 'I don't go to the school CU because I get all the fellowship and teaching I need at my local church'. This is a view
which thinks of my needs rather than my responsibilities. The
school Christian group doesn't exist only for the individual
well-being of Christians. It also exists for witness to the life of
Christ in school. When individual believers cut themselves off
from other Christians, the potential strength of witness is
inevitably decreased. Very often the reason some young people
don't go to the CU is not because they honestly do not feel the
need of what the group has to offer, but because they don't want
to be associated with the cause of Christ in school. The Christian
group also exists for mutual upbuilding and prayer, so that the
corporate witness of that group will be visible and effective.
There may well be Christians in the group who are not so
privileged in the teaching and fellowship they receive in their
churches and they need the encouragement of other believers in
school. One girl, for example, from an Essex village, spoke of her
dependence on the Christian Union as her only real fellowship.
There was no live church in her village and she had no means of
travelling into the nearest town.

Some people have worried that a school CU may see itself as a
church. For a very few groups this has been a real and disruptive
problem; but in most cases young people have no problem in
seeing themselves as members of local Christian fellowships
coming together as Christians in school. Nevertheless, in that
the CU is made up of a group of believers, it is an expression of
the church, and as such it demonstrates the characteristics of a
community of believers, within the context of school. For quite a
number of young people, where there is no lively church in their
area, the school CU does fulfil some of the functions of a local
church, in terms of teaching and fellowship.

A small Christian group was meeting regularly in a rural
school in the Cotswolds. Its members were enthusiastic and

keen to learn more about God and to share him with others. The core of the group was made up of fifth and sixth formers who came from villages scattered over a wide area. Most of them didn't attend a lively church because there wasn't one in their village. Their families may have been traditional church goers, but few had real Christians in their own families. They had been converted in a variety of ways: at Christian camps, to which they returned each year; at a one-off special Christian event in a town some miles away; or through the witness of friends in school. They had no means of travelling to a church in town and had little contact with adult Christians. They were very conscious of their lack of Bible knowledge, yet God had begun to work in their lives. For them, the CU in school was the only regular meeting point with other Christians and in this situation the CU had some of the functions of a local church. For many other young people in both urban and rural areas there is no lively church.

Another reason why the CU is in practice 'church' for some Christians is that the culture of the local church is too different from the world they know for them to feel at home there. A steady flow of people are converted through the witness of school friends. They naturally find it easier to meet at first with other Christians in school in a familiar environment. The jump from this to the formal world of most churches is often too great to contemplate. For them, the CU is an essential bridge to future involvement in a local church.

These two needs – the lack of churches in some rural and urban areas and the problem of the culture gap – present us with a huge challenge. There are many places in our country with no lively fellowship of believers. Do those churches which are well-off – in numbers, money and in spiritual resources – need to consider seriously the need for church planting?

Secondly, do we cling fiercely and inflexibly to our culture rather than the gospel on which our faith is founded? Are we sufficiently in contact with the world of the late twentieth century to communicate the gospel to those who are a part of it and to enable them to feel at ease to worship, fellowship and learn with other believers? Established Christians as well as new converts need to be prepared to make adjustments.

The CU is Baptist!

From time to time a school CU may run into problems because it is dominated by young people from one particular local church. This will probably be for good reasons: the young people from that fellowship are the most enthusiastic or they have more obvious gifts of leadership or perhaps their local church is concerned about school and is praying for them. Problems arise in two areas: one is that teenagers from other local churches feel excluded; the other is that denominational differences of teaching are emphasised. It is, of course, very sad when division arises on either of these two counts and they need to be carefully and sensitively guarded against. The opportunity to share the gospel through life and word with hundreds of unreached young people must not be lost or diminished because of squabbling or offended Christians.

Occasionally, serious differences of opinion arise over extremes that are being emphasised by the more outspoken or over-zealous members. When this is done without respect for the views of other Christians in school, it brings death to the group, not life. Understandably, some Christian parents may advise their teenagers to withdraw. This is a sad loss, both for the individual and for the Christian group which loses the fellowship of one of its members. In this situation much adult support and guidance is needed. Parents, teachers and local ministers need to meet together to talk and pray for their young people. Perhaps if they had done so earlier, the problem wouldn't have arisen.

In one town where a Christian group was meeting regularly in the local school, a new church was established. Young people who had started going to this church wouldn't go to the already existing school CU. They decided it wasn't 'spiritual' enough and so set up their own fellowship group in school without reference to their other brothers and sisters in Christ who were already meeting together. It is hardly surprising that such a circumstance was highly confusing to the rest of the school community. Jesus Christ taught so clearly that the oneness of Christians was a key factor in drawing non-Christians to himself.

When things go wrong in the CU it is easy for adults outside to over-react and perhaps want to close the group down; but as far as possible it is better to encourage perseverance and patience. In the adult Christian world there are squabbles and differences which have to be encountered and dealt with too. We can't just opt out of our family. The Bible teaches that we are to 'Make every effort to keep the unity of the Spirit . . .' (Ephesians 4:3). That suggests it won't always be easy. If the focus of Christian witness is lost in school through the collapse of the CU, then many may not hear the good news about Jesus.

On the brighter side, for most groups the denominational differences amongst the Christians at school don't hinder their essential unity in Christ and in fact they help to enrich the lives of young believers as they encounter people with different backgrounds. In talking about their differences they can help one another to clarify their knowledge and understanding of biblical teaching.

'Meetingitis'

'Meetingitis' is a problem for some long-established groups. The CU programme has been a part of school life for so long that Christian pupils and teachers have forgotten the real reason for meeting. As a result 'going to CU' has become (as can 'going to church') a burden and a monotonous duty. The Christians meet because there is a meeting rather than because they want to meet with each other and God. Or maybe there are too many 'meetings' which prevent Christians from being involved with other school social activities which would allow them to meet the non-Christians they are praying for. Perhaps, even, the large number of meetings is an excuse to avoid non-Christians. Those who are on the outside of Christianity won't be attracted by the group and those who are Christians will want to stay away. Such groups need to stop, take stock and pray for fresh purpose and direction. The temptation is to grind on to the bitter end and then feel resentful towards the Christians who didn't support the meetings of the group.

'It's Boring'

This complaint often goes along with the problem of too many meetings for meetings' sake. It may well be a warning sign to a group whose life, spontaneity and sense of purpose is dwindling.

On the other hand this complaint sometimes arises from a

radically wrong understanding of a school Christian group. It is not about entertainment. 'It's boring' suggests a failed performance. Do you belong to your local church because of its good performances? The school CU is about giving as well as receiving. It is for mutual sharing, encouragement, prayer and resulting witness. That is not to say that believers of all ages shouldn't strive for high standards of presentation and organisation or use their minds creatively to find new ways of helping people to learn and grow.

'It's boring' may also be a response to the kind of people who are in the group, with whom we, perhaps, wouldn't naturally have much in common. But our faith in Christ and life in him supersede this. A fundamental fact of Christianity is that all believers are of great value and equally acceptable in Christ. Our faith needs to be seen to break down all sorts of barriers. Through his people Christ wants to surprise outsiders with his love.

Boredom could also, of course, simply be an excuse for a lack of personal commitment to Christ and other Christians. Whatever the reason, if the CU is boring it is as much my fault and responsibility as anyone else's. God, his world and his purposes are certainly not boring. If the meetings are, then those who feel this, need to make a greater contribution of ideas and commitment to the group. God doesn't allow us to choose our family; he simply puts us in one. These are our brothers and sisters in Christ and our fellow-workers in the gospel. If there is change needed, perhaps we should start with our own attitudes, words and actions.

The greatest task

Towards the beginning of one spring term a Christian group met at their school. Yet again only three or four people had turned up. They looked at one another and felt discouraged. How could they have any impact on the rest of their school with so few of them? They decided to pray that God would increase their numbers, be it through bringing Christians out of the woodwork or through new converts or through uncommitted but interested people coming along. The next week their numbers had doubled. They prayed again. The next week greater numbers came and so it went on. By the end of the term about sixty or seventy people were meeting. In one sense numbers don't matter, but a group of sixty or seventy pupils meeting voluntarily at school is noticed. Most young people like to be a part of a big group. This group were amazed at the way God had answered their prayers.

Prayer is the key to the life and witness of a school Christian group. Through praying about matters directly concerned with their own situation young people find their faith exercised and increased as they see answers; they find their sense of fellowship and enthusiasm growing. Yet many CUs don't pray together, apart from the opening and concluding prayers at a meeting. Instead they get caught up in seeing the CU's activities only in terms of the programme, forgetting God. When any group of Christians stop praying together they lose all sense of God's purposes and of being co-workers with him. Yet, if nothing else, prayer is the task of Christian groups. Christian teenagers are God's people in school. They have opportunities to see, understand and respond to the needs around them which adults outside of school don't have. Intercession for their community is the greatest task they have.

6

The church in school

The challenge

Thousands and thousands of young people today are lost. There is no hope, no future, no purpose. Adults have driven out God-consciousness and the me-centred culture of the late twentieth century is slowly choking its purveyors and victims. No family, no work, no absolutes, no God – these mean no security. In its place there are fear, perversion and pretence.

The church has withdrawn to create its own safe world. We have had such a developed sense of being members of the kingdom that those outside have hardly seemed real – people created in the image of God. Meanwhile our young people have learned to pass from the evangelical culture of Sunday to the world culture of Monday, changing shade to match the background. The two worlds have been kept separate and in practice we have forgotten that Jesus said we were to be *in* the world as members of the kingdom to share what he has given with the hungry.

School, this microcosm of society, is the mission field on the church's doorstep. Christian teenagers and teachers in our fellowships are the workforce for this lost generation. They need to be helped, encouraged, prayed for and given a sense of God's call and an awareness of the possibility that through them God can move in our school communities.

Our response

How then can the local church respond helpfully and practically to the needs and opportunities presented by schools?

Praying for Christian teenagers and their schools

This may sound obvious but many churches do not pray specifically for their local schools.

In one town a group of Christian friends, representing different denominations, decided to meet once a month to pray for the local school. There were no Christian teachers, so any initiative inside school would have to be taken by teenagers. They knew the young Christians in their respective fellowships and encouraged them to establish and run a school Christian Union. The interest of older believers helped to motivate the young people, gave them a sense of involvement in a worthwhile task and the confidence to act, knowing they weren't struggling alone. Also advice was at hand if needed. From time to time one of the CU members would go to the adult prayer group and give a report of what was happening in the CU and in school. They could also share prayer needs in school and any answers to prayers they had seen. The Christian group there still doesn't have vast numbers, but over the last few years the group has consistently made its presence felt: there has been a steady trickle of conversions and the non-Christian staff have looked on with respect and interest.

In an urban area some parents were deeply concerned about their local school, which seemed to them to be a godless and anti-Christian environment. They were afraid for their teenage children and wanted them to be helped to live as Christians at school; and they wanted there to be some felt Christian influence which would bring change to the curriculum and ethos of the school. They began to pray although there didn't seem much hope of change. The head of Religious Education wasn't a Christian; the headmaster was antagonistic to the idea of a CU being started. It was early spring when the group began to meet. By September the headmaster had unexpectedly resigned and a more sympathetic man had taken his place and a young Christian RE teacher who had not previously felt confident enough to run a group, now decided he would try, with the support of the praying parents. At the beginning the group were not allowed to put up posters advertising their meetings and they weren't allowed to run any meetings that could be remotely described as 'evangelistic', but in a quiet way the parents' prayers were answered and a focus for Christian witness and influence in the school had been established.

In one church there were a number of teachers who all taught at a nearby comprehensive. They knew of quite a number of Christian teenagers in the school and longed to see a CU established but felt that the initiative for this should come from the young people themselves. So they agreed to pray that the teenagers would see the need and opportunity to start a CU. Meanwhile the young people talked together and decided they wanted to do just that. Quite unaware of their teachers' prayers, they went to them to ask for help and advice in establishing a Christian Union; and, as a result, a very lively and enthusiastic group was started.

In another school it was the Christian teenagers who decided that they shouldn't be acting alone in school. They felt a part of their local fellowships, but they didn't feel that their local fellowships were aware of the believers in school or of their efforts to be a Christian voice there. So they produced a letter describing the CU and its aims and asked for prayer and practical support. The letter was sent to all the local churches and was very warmly received. Although they hadn't asked for money, many Christians responded by sending gifts. As a result, they were able to put on some special events in school that they wouldn't otherwise have been able to afford. The letter brought an awareness to the local churches of their representatives in school and stimulated regular prayer for them.

Parent prayer groups, inter-church prayer groups, teacher prayer groups: these are some of the numerous ways in which local churches can and are supporting Christians and their witness in school. Other ideas include: prayer in Sunday services for school Christian groups represented in the regular congregation; leaders of CUs – teachers and pupils – being interviewed briefly in Sunday services and prayed for at the beginning of a new school term; a school news spot at the church prayer meeting; prayer requests and news of school CUs featured in the church magazine; a prayer support system for teenagers in the church who are at school – adults could sign up agreeing to give prayer support to one teenager.

Just a Cog or called of God?

Young Christians, and many teachers too, need to know they are called to serve God in school. They need to know that their churches are interested in their school and are in partnership with them in taking a Christian voice into school, this very important and significant part of our community. Young Christians need to be re-educated: missions are not simply done for them; the mission is theirs as representatives of the local church. They need to be given a vision of what God can do through them in other people's lives and a sense of responsibility for the non-Christians they meet each day who never go near a church building but who, nevertheless, live amongst the church.

In youth fellowships made up of school age Christian teenagers, some of the teaching can be specifically related to examples from school; the youth fellowship programme could include a discussion on the problems of being a Christian at school or of school-based witness; during the school holidays practical sessions could be included on ideas for the CU programme or training for leading small Bible study and prayer groups; the youth fellowship meeting could include a regular five minute spot for CU news and prayer for each other; if a special youth event is planned either in an individual church or on an inter-church basis the young people can be challenged and encouraged to invite a non-Christian friend from their school; and encourage the young people themselves to pray both outside and inside school.

In several towns there are inter-school Christian groups of pupils who meet regularly for prayer and fellowship which have grown as a result of encouragement given by adults in local churches.

One of the great features of Mission England was the prayer triplet scheme. This involved three people agreeing to meet regularly to pray for three friends each. Many triplets of young people started praying for their friends and thousands of teenagers made a commitment to Christ before and during the Billy Graham meetings. In several instances new converts have started a Christian group in schools where there was no group before; and there are many schools where the witness of the CU has been greatly strengthened because of new converts and revitalised believers. This has happened, at least in part, because young Christians had a sense of call and responsibility for the non-Christians around them.

Encourage them

Young Christians, more than most, need lots of encouragement, not just formally in services and the church magazine, but through individual members of the adult congregation asking them about life at school and recent CU meetings. This can only happen as information is given and interest aroused. In one town, an inter-church group of adults wanted to find a way of encouraging teenage believers in school and of making local churches aware of what their younger members were doing.

They invited a few representatives from each local church to an evening with pupil representatives from the local school Christian Unions. There were about thirty or forty adults and about ten teenagers aged thirteen to eighteen from six or seven different schools. After a short filmstrip describing some of the pressures on teenagers at school and some of the Christian work going on in school, the young people were interviewed about their experiences of being Christians in school and asked to describe their CU and explain how it worked. For once, the tables were turned, the young were speaking to the adults and telling them of their hopes and struggles in the work of God's kingdom. Many of the adults present didn't usually have much contact with school-age Christians and there was a sense of amazement as these young people spoke – most of them were not very confident or articulate – of their concern for non-Christian friends and of the meetings they organised, of the Bible studies and prayer meetings they regularly led and of speakers they invited into school – all in many cases with little adult help. At the end of the meeting the young people were prayed for. It was by no means just the young people who were encouraged by that evening; the adults were too.

Other ways of raising interest and encouragement from the adult congregation include: a feature article on life at school in the church magazine; a school CU group taking an evening service; a CU programme pinned up on the church noticeboard along with the photographs of young people from the church who are involved in the group.

Be Practical

No matter how great their enthusiasm, most young Christians like to know there is an adult somewhere in the background when it comes to setting up a Christian Union in school. Some schools just don't appear to have any committed Christian teachers. Does that mean that the local church must sit passively by and do nothing? On the contrary, quite a lot can be done from outside. To begin with local churches can get their teenagers together and encourage them to establish a Christian group; they can also give advice on how to do it. Better still someone from the church, for example, a self-employed person, a housewife or anyone else who can be free over lunchtime, can go into school each week to help and support the CU. Contrary to what people think, many headmasters are happy for people to come into school to run voluntary activities. There are many examples of local churches providing help in this way.

One housewife who had left her teaching post when she got married continued to lead a Christian group at the school. She also regularly produced a newsletter for local churches so that they could pray for the school.

In another case two ladies went to a Parent Teacher Association meeting at their children's school and enquired if there were any Christian activities organised for the pupils. The teacher they spoke to said there weren't, but would they like to organise some? They did.

A minister and a member of his congregation from a small village church in East Anglia go to the local school once a week to help the Christian teenagers with their meeting. They give advice on programme planning, suggest speakers and generally act as older leaders alongside the pupil leaders.

One of the great advantages of people from the local church going into school in this way is that a bridge is built between school and the church outside. The young people who go to the CU meeting but who have never gone to church, may well find it easier to start if they've met one or two adults from the local church before.

Perhaps there is already a lively CU in the local school with good teacher support. How else can the church practically show its interest and support and also build bridges between itself and school? One very practical thing is simply to recognise those

Christian teachers who are working very hard on behalf of Christian and non-Christian teenagers in their school and to regard them as set aside for this pastoral and evangelistic work. They need to be freed from other obligations, like teaching in the Sunday School, so that they have enough time to plan and pray for the work of the school CU. This is their service for the local church.

Sometimes a CU would appreciate being able to meet in the more relaxed atmosphere of a home. If there are church members living near the school they could offer their home and hospitality from time to time. This may be for an hour or so after school or – if you're brave enough! – even a whole day. It may not be so nerve-wracking as you think! The leaders of the group always need to get together before each term begins for planning and prayer. Offering your home might encourage them to be more organised and therefore more effective.

Can you offer transport? Sometimes a CU wants to organise a trip to a Christian event which it sees as an evangelistic opportunity. Church members can help by offering transport and may subsidise the cost of tickets for non-Christians who want to go.

Finding speakers for lunchtime CU meetings can be difficult. Are there potential speakers in your congregation who could offer their services? For example, a Christian policeman, doctor or businessman could talk about the difference their faith makes to their job.

Finance is another area where the local church can help. Many Christian teenagers do give for the work of their CU, but they can't afford much. Good publicity, filmstrips, Bible study materials, affiliation to Inter School Christian Fellowship, a variety of speakers, a band for a concert – all of these help make the group's witness more effective in the school and all cost money.

Get involved in School
It is not just the Christians or church-going young people that we need to be concerned for: The local church somehow needs to reach out to the hundreds of teenagers in their local school who have little concept of God. Even though some schools'

environments and curricula do seem only to reinforce secular values, Christians can help to change this.

Church ministers can make informal contact with local headmasters and make it clear that he and the church are ready to offer help where possible and that they are interested in the school and what goes on there. One minister in Essex, having established that kind of relationship with the local school, then offered to put on a voluntary lunchtime service for the school just before Easter. A good number of pupils and staff went.

Christian parents can take an active interest in the school, not just for their child's sake, but for the school as a whole. For example, if the facts of the occult are being taught as part of RE and a number of Christian parents are concerned they could write to the headmaster and if possible go and talk with him and the teacher concerned. If a book which seems unhelpful is being taught in English lessons, then Christian parents can take the lead and tell the school they are not happy. Many parents shy away from talking with school staff about what their children are being taught in the classroom, fearing they will be thought of as troublemakers; but most schools will welcome comments from parents, provided they are reasonable, constructive and not merely critical. As well as expressing anxiety about doubtful areas of the curriculum, Christians need to express approval and thanks for those things which are good. Headmasters are also much more likely to listen to Christians if they are the parents who are willing to do practical jobs for the school, such as raise money for a school swimming pool or offer to help supervise a school trip.

There are two organised opportunities in most schools for parents to meet with teaching staff. One is the parents' evening which is usually held at least once a year. This gives parents the chance to talk about their child's progress and happiness in school with the teachers who have academic and pastoral responsibility for him. The other is the Parent Teacher Association meetings. These also happen regularly and give the opportunity for parents and teachers to share ideas together about what they would like to see happening in their school in a more general way. If all the Christian parents from one area regularly attended such meetings they could have great influence for the good of their local school.

Governing boards of schools often have a place on them for a parent or minister as a governor. These can be powerful positions which Christians, if they are concerned about their young people, need to seek.

Whilst some schools are suspicious of outsiders, many more welcome visitors, seeing in them real value for the pupils as contacts with the wider world. Some local churches have offered their minister or youth leader to take an occasional assembly. Some RE teachers would be very happy for a committed Christian to talk to a class about the reasons for his faith; or they would welcome a member of, say, a Baptist church or Brethren assembly to talk about the way their denomination worships; the RE teacher might even like to bring a class to the church building and have a talk there from the minister or leader of the church.

A major way in which some local churches have responded to the needs and opportunities presented by local schools, is to appoint a full- or part-time local schools worker. Normally the cost of this is carried by a group of local churches whose 'parishes' include a number of schools. As the churches' representative, the local worker can build up a relationship with the different schools. He or she can work regularly with the various Christian Unions giving teaching and training and from time to time helping them to organise a schools' mission week. Often headmasters are glad for someone like this to take regular assemblies and RE teachers may be happy for the local worker to run a course for senior pupils on aspects of the Christian faith over a number of weeks. Appointing someone in this way is obviously a major commitment but can be hugely effective in helping many young people who are outside the church, come in.

Perhaps the commitment needed to appoint a schools worker is too great for your church, but there may well be a full-time worker already covering your area. Some churches may be unaware of the work of Inter School Christian Fellowship, Scripture Union's Schools Department. Scripture Union has a network of regional and local schools workers covering secondary and primary schools in both the state and private sectors in the whole of Britain. They visit schools giving training, teaching and encouragement to Christian pupils and support to Christian teachers. They are involved in schools evangelism, taking RE lessons and assemblies, and are happy to talk with parents, ministers and teachers about the needs in schools and possible responses. Scripture Union also produces material to help school Christian Unions with their programme and organisation.

Your local school may not be visited simply because the Scripture Union worker knows of no Christian contact there. He or she would be glad to meet with people from the local church and work with them in any way possible to take the gospel into the local school. British Youth For Christ also have many schools workers in different parts of the country. The Association of Christian Teachers exists to help teachers, concerned parents, ministers and anyone else who is interested, think through educational issues from a Christian standpoint and to make a distinctively Christian contribution to the school curriculum.

Our responsibility

Are we tempted to look at teenagers and complain about their behaviour, their dress or their standards? Do we look at them and grumble about the state of the world? It is *our* responsibility. They live in the society adults have created. Do we criticise teachers for not keeping control of their classes? It is *our* responsibility. Do we feel our classmates are beyond the help of Christ? It is *our* responsibility.

When Jesus looked out on the crowds just before the feeding of the five thousand, the Bible says that he looked and had compassion on them because they were like sheep without a shepherd (Mark 6:34). That is just how young people are today. We need to be filled with compassion for their pain. We need to repent on behalf of our society which has caused them such hurt. Then we must act to bring them God's revolutionary light and love.

Scripture Union in Schools

Scripture Union local and regional schools workers support, encourage and service more than 2,000 voluntary Christian groups in schools in Britain alone and train many hundreds of Christian young people, as well as adults, in areas of practical discipleship. Most Scripture Union schools staff also take assemblies, and some take R.E. lessons. And SU's schools team are playing a vital role in nurturing young Christians, many of whom will be in the forefront of Christian outreach and service in the years to come.

We are pledged to work alongside local churches and in some areas churches have worked together to back the appointment of a full-time Scripture Union schools worker.

In inner cities SU's schools work is aiming to penetrate schools with new and relevant expressions of Christian discipleship.

And in the holidays Scripture Union offers a full programme of camps, houseparties, community projects and study courses. A camp or houseparty is much more than meetings. It's a Christian community. Young people not only hear Christianity spelt out, they see it lived out.

The task ahead of Scripture Union's schools ministry is immense and urgent. And our resources though growing are still very limited. With a field staff team of forty-five in Britain (plus short term volunteers and associates) we work in primary and secondary schools and in independent boarding schools.

And Scripture Union is active in schools in thirty-five other countries around the world.

For further information write to the Publicity Department, Scripture Union, 130 City Road, London EC1V 2NJ.